LOCALLY BREWED

LOCALLY BREWED

Portraits of Craft Breweries from America's Heartland

ANNA BLESSING

MIDWAY

AN AGATE IMPRINT

CHICAGO

Printed in China.

All photographs copyright © 2014 Anna Blessing

Design by Brandtner Design

Library of Congress Cataloging-in-Publication Data

Blessing, Anna H.
 Locally brewed : portraits of craft breweries from America's heartland / Anna H. Blessing.
    pages cm
 Summary: "A guide to 20 small, Midwestern craft breweries, told through full-color photography, interviews with the brewmasters, and descriptions of their products"--Provided by publisher.
 Includes bibliographical references and index.
 ISBN 978-1-57284-151-2 (pbk.) -- ISBN 1-57284-151-6 (flexibound) -- ISBN 978-1-57284-729-3 (ebook) (print)
 1. Microbreweries--Middle West. 2. Brewers--Middle West--Interviews. I. Title.
 TP573.U6B74 2014
 663'.420977--dc23
                             2013020467

10 9 8 7 6 5 4 3 2 1

Midway Books is an imprint of Agate Publishing. Agate books are available in bulk at discount prices. For more information, go to agatepublishing.com.

For my grandparents,
Barbara Stenger and George Burditt,
who put down roots deep and strong

Table of Contents

INTRODUCTION

IN PART THIS IS A BOOK ABOUT BEER, but mostly it is a book about people: the craftspeople and artisans who brew the beer. Many words have been written about beer; entire books, blogs, and online forums are devoted to the subject. I want to tell the story of the people behind the beer.

Each of the breweries in this book has its place in craft brewing's past, present, or future. I have taken a cross-section of the craft beer movement in the Midwest right at this moment—where it came from, where it is, and where it's going. It is a golden era of craft brewing in the Midwest, and there were so many more breweries I could have included were it not for limitations of time and space. In my hometown of Chicago alone, great places like Revolution, Half Acre, Pipeworks, and Off Color aren't covered in these pages. In the year I spent working on this book, a new brewery was opening somewhere in the country every day. By the end of 2012, there were approximately 2,000 breweries in the country, the highest number since before Prohibition, with an estimated 1,000 on the drawing board for 2013.

My hope is that readers will seek out these and other breweries, take tours, drink beer, eat at the brewpubs, and ask for more suggestions for great local beer along the way.

It's a constantly changing and ever-expanding landscape, and there is so much good craft beer to drink, in the states touching the Great Lakes alone.

A Word on Craft Brewing

It says *craft* on the outside of this book, and I refer to what these brewers are doing as *craft* brewing. But the brewers themselves don't have a unanimous definition of what craft beer is. Many say that to be craft you must be independently owned. Others say that it's about the passion and intention behind the beer. Some call it variety, novelty, extreme. Some brewers scoff at the need to label it at all.

Craft beer can be a brilliantly clean lager or an oak-aged sour beer; it can be a black barley wine or a nutty brown ale; a highly hopped IPA or a beer that can't even be described by anything but its flavors. It's made by people who have a passion for what they do, participating in a community of artisans. Number of barrels, ingredients, and style guidelines—none of these seems to be important. At the end of the day, it's about good beer.

The industry may be booming, but craft brewing isn't a get-rich-quick business. Running a successful brewery takes hard work, passion, science, innovation, control, quality, patience, thick skin, and more often than not, a sense of humor. It also takes time to make good beer. And it takes attention and craft and skill and knowledge. On

the New Glarus Brewing Company website there is a quotation from St. Francis of Assisi: "He who works with his hands is a laborer. He who works with his hands and his head is a craftsman. He who works with his hands, his head, and his heart is an artist." The brewers in this book are artists.

About This Book

Each chapter profiles a Midwestern craft brewery (and one craft cider company), listed in chronological order from oldest brewery to newest, but by no means does this book need to be read from front to back.

I've included a select list of places to Get a Pint, and I encourage you to taste as much beer as you can from these breweries. Many of them have limited distribution, and a few don't distribute outside of their own states. A pilgrimage is in order. The fine drinking establishments listed in each Get a Pint section represent a fraction of the locations where you can order beer produced by each brewer—these lists, in other words, are not meant to be exhaustive in any way.

I've also included a Brewer's Playlist, contributed by the breweries. Early on in my research, I noticed a strong connection between music and brewing. Brewers take their music very seriously, and at breweries where there is more than one brewer working, control of the speakers is usually more competitive than control of the brewhouse.

My hope is the playlists will pair with your drinking, home brewing, or road-tripping across the Midwest.

About Me

My passion is finding and learning about people who have an incredible craft and who are doing what they love. I got the chance to tag along with some of the Midwest's most impressive farmers while writing *Locally Grown: Portraits of Artisanal Farms from America's Heartland*. That journey led naturally to this one. There is an inherent connection between farmers and brewers, sharing interests that include science, art, and hard labor. Plus, many brewers and artisan farmers now work together. Breweries often give farmers spent grain, source unusual and local ingredients from them, and enlist them to grow barley or hops. Some breweries even operate their own farms.

I loved the idea of meeting the people behind the local beer I had been drinking as a resident of Chicago and a sometime resident of northern Michigan. Craft beer is in my blood. I was born and raised in beer utopia Portland, Oregon. And my great, great, great grandfather and his brother, John and Nicholas, were the owners of the Stenger Brewery in Naperville, Illinois, founded in 1848. The brewery made lagers and ales and distributed to saloons in Chicago and beyond until they closed in 1893, feeling the pressure from bigger breweries.

For several years the Stengers employed as its foreman Adolph Coors, until he left abruptly in 1872 for Colorado, where he would start his empire the next year. There are two sides to the story about his sudden departure: One side says that John Stenger had him in mind as a husband for one of his daughters and Adolph, uninterested, departed. The other, that Adolph fell in love with one of the Stenger girls but was jilted and went west. You can guess which side of the story my family tends to tell.

I like to think the breweries opening across Chicago and the Midwest today are continuing in the small, family-owned, independent, local, and regional spirit of places like the Stenger Brewery. And I hope this book sheds some light on these creative craftspeople leading the latest incarnation.

AUGUST SCHELL BREWING COMPANY

NEW ULM, MINNESOTA

Everything about the August Schell Brewing Company says *craft*.

It's the second-oldest family-owned brewery in the country. Owner Ted Marti is a fifth-generation descendant of the company's founder, and today he runs the brewery with his three sons. Production in 2012 was 132,000 barrels. The brewery, located down a picturesque road two miles outside of New Ulm, Minnesota, made it through the Civil War, the Dakota Conflict, Prohibition, both World Wars, the big-brewery takeovers of the 1960s and 1970s, and the craft beer boom and bust of the 1990s.

The Schell family makes the same traditional lagers their ancestors made 150 years ago as well as seasonal and year-round specialty beers based on German-style brews. These include FireBrick, a Vienna-style lager; Pils, a Great American Beer Festival award winner; and Snowstorm, a seasonal release in the spirit of a snowflake (in that no two are the same—brewmasters innovate a new recipe each year).

All these things considered, why is Schell's on the Brewers Association's (BA) list of domestic noncraft breweries, along-side mega noncrafters like Anheuser-Busch and MillerCoors?

The BA, the not-for-profit trade association dedicated to small and independent American craft brewers, issued a

Owner
TED MARTI

Brewmasters
JEREMY KRAL, DAVE BERG

Established
1860

Production Volume
132,000 BARRELS (2012)

Distribution
IOWA
MINNESOTA
NEBRASKA
NORTH DAKOTA
SOUTH DAKOTA
WISCONSIN

Website
schellsbrewery.com

statement in 2012 titled "Craft vs. Crafty," defining the American craft brewer as small, independent, and traditional. The BA also included a list of breweries in the country not considered craft by those standards. The intention was to create transparency and kick out big breweries posing as craft breweries under smaller brands. (Many even go to great lengths to keep their widely recognizable names from being associated with the label brand.)

The BA defined *small* as producing fewer than 6 million barrels a year; none of the breweries in this book produced more than 300,000 barrels a year by 2013. *Traditional* was defined as "a brewer who has either an all-malt flagship or has at least 50 percent of its volume in either all-malt beers or in beers which use adjuncts to enhance rather than lighten flavor." Adjuncts, usually rice or corn, are used by mega breweries to lighten the beer. Because Schell's uses corn in its original Deer Brand beers, which it has done for 150 years, the BA deemed it to be an adjunct user—therefore nontraditional and noncraft.

Jace Marti, Ted's son and sixth-generation Schell's brewer, retorted with a message posted on the brewery's website. In defense of Schell's status as a craft brewery, he wrote that the BA's

> *definition of what makes a traditional brewer, and thus a "craft brewer," comes down to the use of adjuncts. Big brewers often use adjuncts in excess amounts to cut down on brewing costs, and to lighten their beers—the opposite of what the craft beer movement is all about. While this is true for them, it*

Owner Ted Marti with two of his three sons, Franz (center) and
Jace, who are sixth-generation Schell's brewers.

is also a very shortsighted view of brewing in America, and most definitely not
the case for our brewery. When August Schell emigrated from Germany and
founded this brewery in 1860, his only option to brew was to use what was
available to him, as it was impossible to ship large quantities of raw ingredients from Europe at that time. The high-quality, two-row malting barley he
could use back home, wasn't native to North America. Instead, he had to use
the locally grown, but much higher-protein, six-row barley to brew his beer.
When he decided that he wanted to produce a high-quality, clear and stable,
golden lager, he had to cut down that protein content somehow. In order to

accomplish this, he used a small portion of another locally grown ingredient he called "mais" as is hand written in our old brewing logs, better known as corn. He didn't use corn to cheapen or lighten his beer. He did it because it was the only way to brew a high-quality lager beer in America at that point. By the time high-quality, two-row malting barley was finally cultivated and available to use, our consumers had already been drinking our high-quality beers for many years. We continued to brew our beer using this small portion of corn because that was the way we traditionally brewed it.

Pedigree

In 1848 August Schell came to the United States from Durbach, Germany. In 1856 he moved to Minnesota, via Cincinnati, with his wife, two daughters, and a group of Germans who called themselves the Cincinnati Turner Society. Joined by a new settlement of Chicago Germans in southern Minnesota, they formed the town of New Ulm. A few years later, August opened his brewery along the Cottonwood River.

In 1862 the Schells found themselves in the middle of the Dakota Conflict, an uprising of Dakota Sioux Indians in southwest Minnesota. Most of New Ulm was burnt to the ground. The family planned to stay, but the conflict worsened and they left. They returned expecting to see their home and brewery destroyed, but Mrs. Schell had been friendly with the Dakotas, providing them with food and clothing, and the Dakotas had spared them.

August ran the brewery with the help of his two sons, Adolph and Otto, until Adolph moved west and left the brewery operations to Otto and their brother-in-law, George Marti. In 1891 August died and left the brewery to Otto, who ran the brewery until his sudden death in 1911. George Marti, married to August's daughter Emma, took control of the brewery, and since then, ownership has been under the Marti name all the way down to Ted.

Before Prohibition hit in 1919, there were more than 1,900 breweries in the country; New Ulm alone was home to five. Schell's struggled through the dry years, surviving by making nonalcoholic beer and selling candy and pop on its beer routes.

It was one of only 600 breweries that survived after the national ban on alcohol was lifted.

In the late '50s and '60s, a lot of family breweries went out of business. Even the larger regional breweries were eaten up. "The wars ended and everyone was making American lagers," Ted says. "Throwaway cans and bottles, advertising and radio—all these things gave power to the big guys and it got really hard to compete."

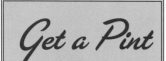

Schell's trudged on through the '60s and '70s. "We always had family who wanted to run the business, we had a local following, we never gave up our own distribution, and we were adaptable," Ted says, citing reasons they were able to survive when many others couldn't.

Schell's hit a low point in 1970, and small breweries across the country were struggling. By that point, the takeover by big breweries had squeezed out competition so that only 31 breweries remained in the United States.

Trying to set itself apart from the big breweries it didn't stand a chance competing against, Schell's started experimenting with full-flavored, heavier beers. The brewery branched out and tried special cans, private-label cans—anything that might mean surviving against the industry giants. It also began to offer production services for smaller breweries and brewers with no ability to produce. Some had nothing, while others had tiny breweries, capable of only 100-barrel batches.

"There were a few people on the coasts brewing," Ted says. "Entrepreneurs who had ideas, but no brewery." In the beginning to the mid-'80s, Schell's brewed for Pete's Wicked Ale, San Andreas Brewing, and Black Dog Ale. Schell's continued contract brewing for other companies through the '90s.

Conscious of Tradition

When Ted took ownership in 1985, craft beer was virtually nonexistent in the Midwest. Trained as a brewmaster at the Siebel Institute of Technology in Chicago, Ted introduced a line of "specialty" beers: alts, pilsners, pale ales, weissbiers.

Vintage hand-hammered copper brewhouse, used from 1895 to 1999; founder August Schell loved the white-tail buck; history is on display in the brewery's museum.

"Since then we've stayed within German-style beers, concentrating on German-style lagers, kölsches, and weissbiers," Ted says.

During its 150-year anniversary celebration, Schell's released its Anniversary Draft Series. In the brewery's extensive archives (Schell's boasts an excellent museum for visitors), a collection of old German recipes for beer were found, including several no longer made today. In 2010 Schell's released eight different beers, including the 1878 Einbecker Doppelbock, the 1905 Vacuum Tonic, and the Hopfenmalz.

Roaming peacocks nibble on trellised hops; Schell's uses specialty malt from Briess Malt and Ingredients in Wisconsin.

Though the draft series was meant to be offered only during the anniversary year, the brewery decided to continue in the same spirit, with its Stag Series of beer. Each Stag beer is a limited release that goes out two to three times a year.

Schell's also brews six year-round and seven seasonal beers, including a blonde doppelbock; an Oktoberfest; a kölsch; and amber, dark, and black lagers. Its original Deer Brand—an American lager the brewery has made since before Prohibition—and the Grain Belt brand beers are made with corn. (These are the beers that triggered the controversy with the BA.)

In 2001 Schell's bought Grain Belt Brewery, a Minneapolis brewery with a history nearly as long as Schell's. Originally produced in 1893, Grain Belt was the flagship beer of Minneapolis Brewing Company, which eventually changed its name to match

Aromatic hops pellets, ready for brewing.

its popular beer. Even as a successful, larger regional brewery, Grain Belt couldn't compete with the national breweries in the '70s. The failing company was sold to G. Heileman Brewing Company in Wisconsin. Heileman moved the brewery first from Minneapolis to St. Paul, and then from St. Paul to La Crosse, Wisconsin. Financial problems followed Grain Belt and its series of owners, until Schell's finally bought it. Now Schell's brews three Grain Belt beers in addition to its Schell's brand beers.

By 2012 beer production at Schell's was maxed out at 132,000 barrels. Plans for a $2 million expansion would double production capacity for 2014.

Because of many factors—the purchase of Grain Belt, the release of innovative styles, and the sustained production of quality German-style beer—Schell's has made it well into the 21st century.

A Future Built on the Past

A narrow and winding road takes you through the woods and onto the grounds of the brewery. August Schell's picturesque retirement home, built in 1885, is still surrounded by well-maintained gardens and a deer park. The brewery's resident peacocks nibble on trellised hops. The light is bright, the air is clear, and it's easy to believe you've arrived in a small German town overflowing with fresh beer.

Jace studied in Berlin and spent time working at small breweries in Germany. In an unused outdoor space on the brewery grounds, he hopes to add a beer garden. He and his brothers will be the ones to take over Schell's from their father, becoming the brewery's sixth generation of family ownership. From the looks of it, they're well equipped to lead the brewery into the next century as a historic, family-owned craft brewery.

BELL'S BREWERY, INC.

KALAMAZOO AND COMSTOCK, MICHIGAN

hen you walk into Bell's shiny new brewery, the 200-barrel Huppmann copper kettles are glowing, light is flooding in from the tall windows, and the floors look like they've just been scrubbed. When it's empty, it is a quiet, calm, and serene space. As Laura Bell, daughter of founder Larry Bell, says, "It's like when you walk into a church cathedral when nobody is in there."

Bell's has come a long way from a 15-gallon soup pot.

Then/Now

It's hard to have a conversation about craft beer in the Midwest and not inevitably come to Larry Bell at some point. And it might be safe to say that there isn't a Midwest brewer today who hasn't tipped his hat to Larry and marveled at what he has done.

Before Larry opened the brewery, he was working at Sarkozy bakery in downtown Kalamazoo, Michigan, alongside a baker who was also a homebrewer. Surrounded by bread and yeast every day at the bakery and fascinated with the idea of fermentation, Larry decided to give brewing a shot. It turned out he was pretty good at it.

People around him were excited about having something to drink other than fizzy yellow beer, and he started homebrewing—with a 15-gallon stockpot—for friends and a growing

Owner
LARRY BELL

Brewmaster
JOHN MALLETT

Established
1985

Production Volume
216,000 BARRELS (2012)

Distribution
ALABAMA / ARIZONA
FLORIDA / GEORGIA
ILLINOIS / INDIANA
IOWA / KENTUCKY
MICHIGAN / MINNESOTA
MISSOURI / NORTH CAROLINA
NORTH DAKOTA / OHIO
PENNSYLVANIA / PUERTO RICO
SOUTH CAROLINA / VIRGINIA
WASHINGTON DC / WISCONSIN

Website
bellsbeer.com

circle of fans. The story goes that one night he was in his basement bottling when there was a knock on his door. Larry panicked, thinking it must be the feds coming to shut him down. There is a federal limit on how much you can homebrew, and he had far surpassed that. It turned out it was just a local bluegrass band coming to pick up a case before going out on tour. After his scare, Larry decided to make it legal.

In 1983 he started Kalamazoo Brewing Company, a homebrew store, where he sold supplies while getting his brewery together. He was ready to open in 1985, at 26 years old. He brewed 185 barrels the first year. "The beer wasn't very good back then," Larry laughs. "But we went from that to 216,000 barrels, in 27 years."

Any craft brewer will tell you it isn't about size, but it is still an impressive marker of the progress Bell's has made since its humble beginnings. The Brewers Association released a list of the top 50 breweries in the country based on beer production volume and sales in 2011, with Anheuser-Busch and MillerCoors coming in at first and second. Bell's was listed at thirteenth—behind big-craft guys including Sierra Nevada and New Belgium, but bigger in size than Harpoon, Lagunitas, Stone, Dogfish Head, and Brooklyn Brewery.

It has an unusual position in the craft-brewing world: Bell's is very large in comparison to breweries producing up to tens of thousands of barrels, but it's still very small with respect to other, larger breweries still considered craft (Sierra Nevada produces 1 million barrels a year). Bell's growth isn't slowing, but the family likes to hang on to its roots as a very small, local craft brewery. "When people walk in and say, 'Oh man! I had no idea Bell's was so big,' that's what we are striving for," Laura says.

But the facts are, Bell's is big. It has a 35,000-square-foot distribution center, a pub in downtown Kalamazoo, and a production volume of 216,000 barrels in 2012; its 2013 production projection was 260,000 barrels. Along with the brewery's

TODAY'S DRAFT BEER LIST

THIRD COAST (ON NITRO) ... CREAMY, EARTHY SLIGHT BITE 4.8% ... TWO HEARTED OUR STAPLE IPA 7% ... DAGGER STOUT DRY, IMPERIAL FULL BODY 10.3%

...MAN LIGHT SESSION WHEAT 4% ... RED NOSE ESB CARAMEL NOTES w/ PINEY AROMAS ... EXPEDITION STOUT IMPERIAL, RICH + COMPLEX NOTES 10.5%

BEST BROWN LIGHT MALT w/ CARAMEL NOTES 5.8% ... MILD ALE LIGHT, EARTHY AMBER 3.8% ... BLACK NOTE STOUT 12 OZ POUR ONLY!

THIRD COAST LIGHT AMERICAN PALE 4.8% ... HARVEST ALE 100% MICHIGAN MALTS 5.7% ... KAL-HAVEN RYE ALE w/ BRETTANOMYCES 6.8%

PALE ALE FLORAL, HERBAL HOP 5.2% ... LAGER OF THE LAKES LIGHT, CRISP, PILSNER 5.0% ... MILK STOUT SMOOTH + SWEET, MADE w/ LACTOSE 5%

WINTER WHITE SEASONAL BELGIAN INSPIRED WHEAT 5.5% ... WILD ONE SOUR BROWN ALE 6.6% ... MEAD STRONG HONEY WINE 9.8%

... TRUMPETERS STOUT DRY IRISH STYLE 4.0% ... HOPSLAM HUGE CITRUS NOTES, DIPA 10%

Get a Pint

ECCENTRIC CAFÉ

Kalamazoo, Michigan

bellsbeer.com

••••

OLD BURDICK'S BAR & GRILL

Kalamazoo, Michigan

oldburdicks.com

••••

LOCAL OPTION

Chicago, Illinois

localoptionbier.com

••••

MARIA'S PACKAGED GOODS & COMMUNITY BAR

Chicago, Illinois

community-bar.com

Bell's runs the Eccentric Café, which offers 20 fresh beers on tap, including hard-to-find specialties and seasonals like Hopslam and Expedition Stout.

$20 million expansion in 2012, it hired 84 people. The new facility is capable of producing as many as 600,000 barrels a year. "It's quickly becoming a lot of beer," Laura says.

Laura has been working at the brewery full time for more than five years, and she is the second-largest owner behind her father. "I'm two months older than the brewery, and I've been around here my whole life," Laura says. She started in sales, and then worked through nearly every department in the brewery before she took on the role of director of marketing.

Larry can't quite say how he did what he did. "I didn't make any money—Laura's mother had a job. I worked seven days a week and eked by," he says. But he had seen what was happening on the West Coast with beer and thought that people were going to catch on in the Midwest. By 1990 they did, and things began to change.

Being Larry

A couple of years ago during a company-wide survey, the Bell's HR department asked employees, "What is Larry's job?" The staff replied, "Larry's job is to be Larry."

Larry gets excited when he sees strangers wearing Bell's T-shirts; because they're only available online and at the Bell's shop in Kalamazoo, he knows he is meeting a true fan. Once he was at a Chicago Cubs game when he introduced himself to a Bell's T-shirt-wearer. The guy said, "If you were Larry Bell, you'd have a business card made of wood." Larry's cards are indeed printed on two-ply sheets of a variety of woods, including a sweet-smelling Eastern Red Cedar. Larry produced a card as proof for the Bell's enthusiast.

If you ask Larry what he does today, he says he bounces between things: dealing with the politics of the business, traveling to meetings and conferences, working with the banks and the lawyers, and, well, being Larry. If you ask Laura, she says, "When you need a name for a beer or a recipe for a beer, you call Larry." Although recipes and names aren't solely his domain, staffers still defer to him for ideas. And if you ask him whether he brews for fun anymore, Larry smiles politely and says, "I have very qualified people and I let them do their job." But with a little pushing, the homebrewer in him comes out. "Oh, sometimes I go up to my cottage up north and get buzzed and put on my old records and start writing recipes," he says, with a little wink in his smile.

He might not be mashing in anymore, but Larry still likes hunting down unusual ingredients and working with Michigan farmers. Bell's owns an 80-acre farm in Shepherd, Michigan, where it grows two-row barley. This barley is malted and used in Bell's beer, including its Christmas ale, which is made entirely using this Michigan barley. Bell's renamed its pale ale from Bell's Pale Ale to Bell's Midwestern Pale

Regular tours are given at the Comstock brewery, where visitors can see and smell the variety of Briess malts used in Bell's beer.

Ale, also brewed with barley. Larry works with an organic six-row-barley grower in the Upper Peninsula as well as with local hop farmers. He and his brewers make a harvest ale using 100 percent Michigan malt and hops, and they buy local Michigan

honey for Hopslam and Michigan cherries for their cherry stout. "Farming is such a big part of Michigan's agricultural heritage— it's nice to be able to be a part of that," Laura says.

Larry is also actively involved in supporting the local arts. He's on the board of the Kalamazoo Institute of Arts, and the brewery has done arts underwriting and fundraising for places like the Kalamazoo Institute of Arts, the Gilmore Keyboard Festival, and the Kalamazoo Symphony.

"What he is not telling you is that he is always reading poetry, listening to all kinds of music, playing a couple of different

Two Hearted Ale

BELL'S

BREWED AND BOTTLED BY
BELL'S BREWERY, INC., COMSTOCK, MI 49053

instruments—a lot of his support of the arts is because of his personal interests," Laura says.

From the beginning, Larry has always been the artist and the businessman; his skill as both attributes to the success and staying power of Bell's. "It's such a mix between art and entrepreneurship," Laura says. "You get to be an artist and play around with flavors and recipes, but you need to have the business side too. A lot of these pioneers have both."

While some in the beer world believe there is plenty of room for craft to continue to grow at its rapid pace, Laura and Larry say they think the market is going to get saturated—quickly. In 2013 there were four new breweries opening in Kalamazoo alone. Larry points out that there are a finite number of tap handles and a limited amount of shelf space and that "those big guys aren't exactly rolling over and saying, 'Go ahead, take our spot.'" Some breweries will hang around for 20 years; but others will go belly up quickly, he says.

Larry has some words of wisdom to the young. "Don't have delusions of grandeur, like 200,000 barrels the first year," he says. "It's taken [us] 30 years. It's a lot of work, and your beer better be amazing."

LAKEFRONT BREWERY, INC.

MILWAUKEE, WISCONSIN

ong before the organic food movement took hold in the Midwest, Russ Klisch introduced the nation's first USDA-certified organic beer. Lakefront has been brewing its organic beer with organic hops since 1996.

Nearly 10 years later, Anheuser-Busch and two smaller breweries joined together to convince the USDA to rule that organic hops needn't be required for organic beer. Russ put up a fight. "They're less than 5 percent of the ingredients, when you consider water, but they are 50 percent of the taste and the flavor," Russ says. "It doesn't make sense to brew organic beer with nonorganic hops."

Lakefront kept working with organic farmers to source hops, and in the meantime, Russ wrote a few letters to the government in an effort to overturn the ruling. He testified before the USDA on behalf of the hop farmers, and his efforts were successful: as of 2013 organic hops are mandated to make organic-certified beer.

The Beginning

Competition has always driven innovation, and Lakefront started with some friendly brotherly competition. In 1981 Jim Klisch expressed interest in brewing beer, and his brother Russ bought him a brewing book for his birthday. To Russ's surprise, Jim not only read the book but also brewed the beer—and it was pretty good.

Owner
RUSS KLISCH

Head Brewer
LUTHER PAUL

Established
1987

Production Volume
33,370 BARRELS (2012)

Distribution
ALASKA / ARIZONA
CALIFORNIA / COLORADO
CONNECTICUT / FLORIDA
GEORGIA / HAWAII / IOWA
IDAHO / ILLINOIS / INDIANA
KANSAS / MAINE / MARYLAND
MASSACHUSETTS / MICHIGAN
MINNESOTA / MISSOURI / MONTANA
NEBRASKA / NEVADA / NEW JERSEY
NEW YORK / NORTH CAROLINA
OHIO / OKLAHOMA / OREGON
PENNSYLVANIA / RHODE ISLAND
SOUTH CAROLINA / SOUTH DAKOTA
TENNESSEE / VIRGINIA
WASHINGTON / WASHINGTON DC
WISCONSIN

Website
lakefrontbrewery.com

Lakefront's My Turn series gives all employees a turn at the brewhouse. Fifty barrels of the one-off beer are bottled and given a personalized label for the guest brewer.

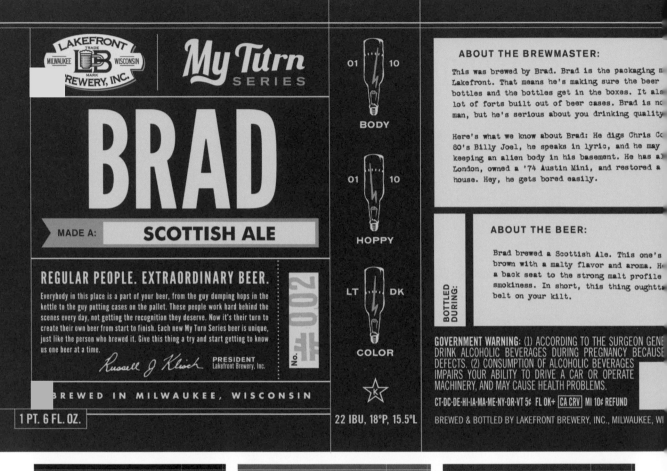

LAKEFRONT BREWERY, INC.

MILWAUKEE · WISCONSIN

My Turn SERIES

BRAD

MADE A: SCOTTISH ALE

REGULAR PEOPLE. EXTRAORDINARY BEER.

Everybody in this place is a part of your beer, from the guy dumping hops in the kettle to the guy putting cases on the pallet. These people work hard behind the scenes every day, not getting the recognition they deserve. Now it's their turn to create their own beer from start to finish. Each new My Turn Series beer is unique, just like the person who brewed it. Give this thing a try and start getting to know us one beer at a time.

Russell J Klisch

PRESIDENT
Lakefront Brewery, Inc.

BREWED IN MILWAUKEE, WISCONSIN

1 PT. 6 FL. OZ.

01 — 10
BODY

01 — 10
HOPPY

LT — DK
COLOR

22 IBU, 18°P, 15.5°L

ABOUT THE BREWMASTER:

This was brewed by Brad. Brad is the packaging m
Lakefront. That means he's making sure the beer
bottles and the bottles get in the boxes. It als
lot of forts built out of beer cases. Brad is no
man, but he's serious about you drinking quality

Here's what we know about Brad: He digs Chris Co
80's Billy Joel, he speaks in lyric, and he may
keeping an alien body in his basement. He has al
London, owned a '74 Austin Mini, and restored a
house. Hey, he gets bored easily.

ABOUT THE BEER:

Brad brewed a Scottish Ale. This one's
brown with a malty flavor and aroma. He
a back seat to the strong malt profile
smokiness. In short, this thing oughtta
belt on your kilt.

BOTTLED DURING:

GOVERNMENT WARNING: (1) ACCORDING TO THE SURGEON GENE
DRINK ALCOHOLIC BEVERAGES DURING PREGNANCY BECAUSE
DEFECTS. (2) CONSUMPTION OF ALCOHOLIC BEVERAGES
IMPAIRS YOUR ABILITY TO DRIVE A CAR OR OPERATE
MACHINERY, AND MAY CAUSE HEALTH PROBLEMS.

CT-DC-DE-HI-IA-MA-ME-NY-OR-VT 5¢ FL OK+ CA CRV MI 10¢ REFUND

BREWED & BOTTLED BY LAKEFRONT BREWERY, INC., MILWAUKEE, WI

My Turn SERIES

DAN

MADE A: BALTIC PORTER

REGULAR PEOPLE. EXTRAORDINARY BEER.

37 IBU, 19°P, 40°L

1 PT. 6 FL. OZ.

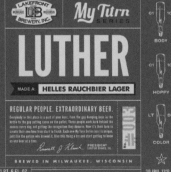

My Turn SERIES

LUTHER

MADE A: HELLES RAUCHBIER LAGER

REGULAR PEOPLE. EXTRAORDINARY BEER.

20 IBU, 13°P, 9°L

1 PT. 6 FL. OZ.

My Turn SERIES

CHAD

USDA ORGANIC

MADE A: BARLEY WINE STYLE ALE

REGULAR PEOPLE. EXTRAORDINARY BEER.

74 IBU, 25°P, 17°L

1 PT. 6 FL. OZ.

Russ thought, "If my brother can make a good beer, I can probably brew a better one." They both started making beer regularly and entering it in contests. Jim would win an award, Russ would win the next, and then Jim would win the next. Eventually they combined talents and opened a brewery together, establishing Lakefront in 1987. The brothers started with three beers: Eastside Dark, Klisch Pilsner, and Riverwest Stein. Production was five barrels in the first year (granted, they opened in December). For a quarter-century the brewery grew steadily, innovating from the start. By 2012 Lakefront was producing 33,370 barrels.

A History of Firsts

In addition to crafting the first government-certified organic beer, Lakefront lays claim to releasing the first fruit beer since Prohibition—a cherry lager released in 1992—as well as the only commercially brewed pumpkin lager in the world when it came out in 1989. And in 2006 it made the first government-certified gluten-free beer—New Grist, brewed with sorghum, rice, and gluten-free yeast.

Lakefront proved to be a pioneer and grew to be a reliable Midwestern brewery. But as the market began to flood with other innovative craft breweries in 2009, 2010, and 2011, Russ realized it had to re-establish itself—this time in the modern market. That meant continuing to innovate in the way it always had, but it also meant doing things like one-offs and bigger beers, something Lakefront traditionally hadn't brewed.

The My Turn series is one example of this diversification. All employees in the brewery, whether they've ever set foot in a brewhouse or not, get the chance to design and brew a namesake beer. Lakefront produces 50 barrels of the beer and then it's done. Dan—Lakefront's tax-compliance guy, shipping manager, and employee of more than 20 years—started out the project with a bang. He made a Baltic porter from an old homebrew recipe: a beer so good it won a bronze at the World Beer Cup in 2010. Chad, an organic barley wine, and Brad, a Scottish ale, were two others in the series.

Along with reasserting itself as a competitive, creative brewery in its out-of-state markets, Russ wanted to make Lakefront first and foremost Milwaukee's craft beer.

Indigenous Ingredients

Russ's longtime support of small, local farmers has resulted in some of Lakefront's other new and inspired brews, including Local Acre, 100 percent of whose hops and malt come from Wisconsin.

In 2012 Lakefront took it one step further. It brewed another Local Acre beer, but this time it was a wet-hopped version. And Lakefront shared the same fresh hops with four other Wisconsin breweries—Central Waters Brewing, South Shore Brewery, Bull Falls Brewery, and Sprecher Brewing—to create a collection of distinct styles and different labels.

The Wisconsinite, a summer hefeweizen, is made with all local ingredients—including indigenous

yeast. "American brewers have really pushed the hop and still are," Russ says. "But I think yeast is sort of the unexplored frontier of American brewing."

Lakefront worked with a storeowner of a Northern Brewer Homebrew Supply who used locally grown grain to propagate yeast samples. The samples were sent to White Labs, a company that manufactures yeast for brewers, and that narrowed it down to two possible strains.

One was a wild *Brettanomyces*-like yeast that was extremely unpredictable. The other was close to a hefeweizen ale yeast with clove and citrus flavors. And that determined the beer.

Running a Marathon

As the owner of one of the older craft breweries in the Midwest, Russ has the perspective of more than two decades of beer. "Wisconsin is blessed and cursed by how frugal we are, and brewing is one example where being frugal helped," he says. "Everybody

Russ Klisch says operating a brewery is like running a marathon, not a sprint.

here bought a bunch of junk and made a brewery out of it—including myself—so there was never a huge overhead." Russ says he has always been cautious with growth, increasing sales steadily.

As Lakefront moved forward, many other breweries around it failed, including Franconia Brewing Company of Mount Pocono, Pennsylvania, which sold Lakefront its copper, Huppmann-manufactured brewhouse when it shuttered its doors after doing business for approximately six months. The new brewery had raised 2 million dollars in 1996—an especially large amount of money to start a brewery at the time. To survive, the owners had to produce 10,000 barrels of beer from the start. "They made 5,000, which isn't bad, and they made great beer," Russ says. "But you're running a marathon, not a sprint."

BREWER'S PLAYLIST

NOTORIOUS B.I.G. • Gimmie the Loot
BLACK SABBATH • The Wizard
DAVID BOWIE • Suffragette City
JAMES BROWN • Get Up Offa That Thing
GARY NUMAN • Cars
YAZ(OO) • Situation
BIZ MARKIE • Vapors
PRINCE • Pussy Control
THE CLASH • Rock the Casbah
VARIOUS ARTISTS • She's Too Fat Polka
JACKSON 5 • The Love You Save
SNOOP DOGGY DOGG • Ain't No Fun
WISHBONE ASH • The King Will Come
ELECTRIC WIZARD • Dopethrone
MASTODON • Blood and Thunder
THE DOORS • Break on Through (To the Other Side)
JIMI HENDRIX • Voodoo Child (Slight Return)
BLACK SABBATH • Children of the Grave
THE MELVINS • The Bit

As far as the term *craft beer*, Russ thinks *artisanal* might be a more fitting word. He says he thinks of beer in terms of music: there is a guy who is a musician but only plays weddings, and then there is a guy who plays his own music and wants to be who he wants to be. "That's craft," Russ says, "somebody sitting there, trying to come up with something unique and different."

With beer, he says, it's ultimately up to the customer to decide if a brewery is doing something different or taking a new angle, but as a small brewer he believes that has to be the goal. "The big guys are imitators, not innovators; if you're a craft brewery, you have to be some kind of innovator," Russ says. "Otherwise you're just playing the wedding music."

GREAT LAKES BREWING COMPANY

CLEVELAND, OHIO

"D on't let me forget to tell you about the Sumerian Beer Project," says Pat Conway, co-owner of Great Lakes Brewing Company in Cleveland, Ohio.

It's unlikely he will forget: it has become a passion project turned to near obsession. It all started when Pat walked through the archaeological wing of the Oriental Institute at the University of Chicago, wanting to learn about the link between beer and the Sumerians, the dominant culture of Mesopotamia in the third and second millennia BC.

Breweries have made beers inspired by ancient flavors and ingredients, such as Dogfish Head's Midas Touch and Anchor's Ninkasi. But Pat had a new idea: "Why don't we replicate exactly the way the Sumerians would have done it with the same equipment and be totally off the grid with no stainless steel, no refrigeration, using the equipment they would have used?"

The U of C archaeologists jumped on the idea. University pottery students crafted brewing vessels based on unearthed chards of pottery believed to have been used for brewing. Great Lakes brewers used them to begin to replicate the ancient beer as it had been brewed—only without a recipe.

"They never left a recipe," Pat says. "They have voluminous notes from government documents: who bought it, what they paid for it, how much they paid for it, the raw materials, but no one knows how they made it."

Owners
PATRICK AND DANIEL CONWAY

Established
1988

Production Volume
132,000 BARRELS (2012)

Distribution
ILLINOIS
INDIANA
KENTUCKY
MICHIGAN
MINNESOTA
NEW JERSEY
NEW YORK
NORTH CAROLINA
OHIO
PENNSYLVANIA
VIRGINIA
WASHINGTON DC
WEST VIRGINIA
WISCONSIN

Website
greatlakesbrewing.com

Great Lakes has spent a year trying to make the beer, avoiding anachronisms as best as it can. Brewers have yet to make a viable version, but Pat continues to pursue the project with undying devotion.

He has in front of him a lengthy email from a University of Chicago archaeologist on a dig in Afghanistan, with whom he has been writing about ingredients and plans for moving forward with the beer. In an exchange with the archaeologist, Pat was still seeking the most authentic path to the brew with fervor when he wrote and asked: "Is there a value in setting out a petri dish with honey in Iraq to grab yeast?"

Full-Bodied Beers

When Pat was in graduate school at the University of Chicago in the late '70s, he worked nights at Jim Sheedy's. "I used to sell a lot of imported beer, and I thought there had been a change in the American palate that American breweries hadn't responded to," Pat says. "Americans were now looking for more full-bodied beers: porters and stouts and more flavorful lagers."

Out of school, Pat taught history at an inner-city school in Chicago for several years and worked as a social worker for the circuit court. When he left to return to his hometown of Cleveland, he decided to pursue the idea of opening a brewery. His brother, Dan, a loan officer at a Cleveland bank, helped him formulate the business plan before quitting the bank to become a partner. They started the brewery as a restaurant, with the idea to grow and eventually make beer for the Great Lakes region.

The Conway brothers looked all over the city and decided on a series of boarded-up buildings in a sketchy neighborhood. The four historic spaces had once been a livery studio, a bar, a feed store, and a silver-dollar saloon with an upstairs burlesque house. The bar proved to be a good choice: it housed a beaten-up tiger mahogany bar from 1860 that restored beautifully. But it wasn't until they'd pulled down all

the boards on the outside that they realized they were meant to be there. On the exterior brick façade a sign was painted: "Lloyd & Keys Old Stock, Kennett Ales & Porters on draught, for family and medicinal purposes." Lloyd and Keys once brewed beer in Cleveland before the turn of the century; proof that earlier drinkers had been enjoying bigger, more full-bodied ales. "That sign was like Ahab beckoning us," Pat says.

Historic Roots

Pat and Dan are an unusual example of craft brewery founders: they weren't brewers themselves. "I homebrewed one time, and it was awful," Pat says. But Pat's passion for history has been part of the beers and what Great Lakes has done from the beginning.

The first brewer they hired was a retired brewmaster who had worked for a big million-barrel brewery. The brewer went on to brew the Dortmunder Gold, Great Lakes' first beer, which won a gold medal at the Great American Beer Festival. (The

beer was originally called the Heisman after John Heisman, of football and trophy
fame, because his home was across from the brewery. Pat and Dan renamed it when
the Downtown Athletic Club in New York, which gives out the trophy, sent a cease-
and-desist letter.)

Eliot Ness, a Vienna-style lager, and Burning River Ale, a pale ale, followed. After
Eliot Ness put Al Capone in jail in Chicago, he went to Cleveland and ran the police
and fire departments. Ness used to frequent the original bar where the Great Lakes bar
is now, and Pat attributes the few bullet holes they've found to his one-time presence
there. (Another layer to the story is that Pat and Dan's mother worked as a stenogra-
pher and used to take dictations from Ness.)

Burning River Pale Ale was named for the
notable 1969 fire on Cleveland's Cuyahoga River,
which captured the nation's attention and spurred an
environmental movement. Every summer the brewery hosts the Burning River Fest to raise money
for the environmental community. Great Lakes has
raised and donated more than $300,000 to date.

The Edmund Fitzgerald, one of the most deco-
rated porters in the country with 16 awards, is
named for the American Great Lakes freighter that
sank in a Lake Superior storm in 1975. Conway's
Irish Ale has a photograph of the Conway brothers'
grandfather, Patrick Conway, a police officer who
used to direct traffic down the street. The Wright
Pils, a classic German pilsner, is named for the
Wright brothers.

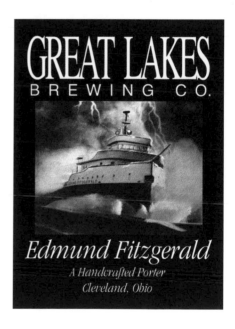

"You had the Wright brothers in Dayton, Thomas Edison in Toledo, Henry Ford in
Detroit, Andrew Carnegie in Pittsburgh—this was the heartland of innovation before
the turn of the century," Pat says. Great Lakes continues to celebrate a history of innovators—and to innovate itself.

25 Years

Pat says he and Dan run the brewery with the Japanese concept of *kaizen* in mind: the concept of constantly striving for quality and excellence with the idea that you will never get there.

As an example of this practice, they hosted a company-wide summit, when they closed the brewery for three days and everyone got in a room together. "We asked, where have we been, where are we now, and where do we want to go," Pat recalled. "Everyone's opinion had value—from the brewers to the bartenders to the truck drivers."

Pat says the brewery has been successful as a result of the culmination of many things: attention to detail; buying the best ingredients; hiring brewers who love the trade; the staff's *esprit de corps*; and, above all, the staff-wide attention to quality of service, food, atmosphere, and, of course, beer.

Every beer is labeled with a drink-by date. Edmund Fitzgerald has a shelf life of 180 days; the IPA, 90 days. Great Lakes sends quality control staff into the field to hunt down and pull expired beer. "We are trying to get people to think differently about beer; it's a perishable project," Pat says.

Another way to ensure Great Lakes beer is kept fresh is to limit its distribution to the Midwest. "Sixty-five percent of the US population is within 500 miles of Cleveland," Pat notes. "Why would we try to sell nationally or internationally when we can keep it local and fresh?"

Great Lakes beer does, however, make its way outside of its distribution. Great Lakes has an outpost at the Cleveland airport. Delayed travelers have been known to tweet, "Best layover ever!" along with a picture of a Great Lakes sampler. Recently it occurred to Pat: if you can get on board with a bottle of scotch, why not a six-pack to go? Now travelers can carry on six-packs of Great Lakes.

One day, an airport bar customer was commenting to the bartender how extraordinary the beer was, and the bartender mentioned he could buy six-packs to take home. When the customer finished his beer, paid, and walked away, she figured she had lost the sale. But soon he returned; he'd gone to buy luggage to carry the beer home.

The Triple Bottom Line

Pat takes pride in the company's triple bottom line: social, economic, and environmental sustainability, which is represented in the logo's three wavy lines.

"Everyone has a financial bottom line, but not a social and environmental bottom line," Pat says. "We are trying to define the metrics, in order to take it seriously and measure progress."

Great Lakes operates two farms, including the largest contiguous acreage of urban farming in the country: the one-acre Pint Size Farm across the street from the brewery. Great Lakes grows a variety of vegetables as well as hops it uses for beer brewed in the small brewpub systems. Vegetables from the farms go to the restaurant.

The pub has a locally focused menu: it gives spent barley to a farmer who raises cattle for its hamburger. The pub pretzels are made by an artisan baker who uses the spent grain. Bottling mistakes even get reused and sent to an ice cream maker, who has made a chocolate chip–porter ice cream and a Christmas Ale ice cream for the restaurant.

The filter sheets from brewing go to a worm farm, and all plastic, including scraps, is recycled. At the end of the day the brewery has an incredibly small annual bill for its dumpster: less than $1,000. Solar panels on the roof help heat the water. Great Lakes is committed to 1% for the Planet and giving back to groups that work in the arts or sustainability.

"Building this brewery was as much about urban renewal as establishing one of the finest breweries in the country," Pat says. When he and Dan first opened their brewery, the neighborhood was pretty rough-and-tumble. The landlord wasn't going to rent them the space, saying he was waiting for the neighborhood to change to sell. "I told him he needed a change agent for the neighborhood to change," Pat says. "We were the change agent."

NEW GLARUS BREWING COMPANY

NEW GLARUS, WISCONSIN

The New Glarus Brewing Company campus is one of a kind. It starts with the exterior, reminiscent of a Swiss chalet in the mountains, and continues inside and throughout the entire brewery—up to the shiny copper brewhouse vessels and down a hallway where panes of glass are held in modern stainless steel. The thick panes are windows that look into the fermentation and finishing cellar and the packaging hall. All breweries have a brewhouse, fermenters, packaging lines. But none looks like New Glarus.

The 65-foot-tall stainless steel fermenters aren't on legs, like most are; they're suspended in a system that makes them easier to clean and better for workers. Three miles of stainless steel pipe run around and through the fermenters, with 1,400 contact points that open and shut valves; a user-friendly system that is also visually striking. Floors are painted deep red, the trusses are green, and everything else is glass, stainless steel, and grey. Every piece of the brewery's design pays attention to both function and aesthetic.

Smaller craft brewers visiting New Glarus have said to founder and president Deb Carey, "My brewery costs less than your landscape." But if they knew the story, they'd appreciate how New Glarus got to where it is today—with nothing but hard work and creativity.

Founder & President
DEB CAREY

Brewmaster
DAN CAREY

Established
1993

Production Volume
144,000 BARRELS (2013)

Distribution
WISCONSIN

Website
newglarusbrewing.com

Working for Others

Deb and Dan Carey met in 1983 working at a microbrewery in Montana. Dan, one of the youngest brewmasters in the country, was working in rough conditions. He brewed in an un-air-conditioned area, working more than 100 hours a week brewing, welding tanks, and cleaning. From the beginning, he was making really good beer—beer aficionado and writer Michael Jackson wrote an article saying Dan made the best bock in Northern America. But he was overworked, making $16,000 a year, with no overtime or health insurance.

The couple got to a breaking point when, living in a single-wide trailer with broken pipes and trying to raise their new baby, they couldn't even count on their checks to go through. Dan applied for a scholarship at the Siebel Institute of Technology, which he received, and they packed up and moved to Chicago.

The next 10 years took them all over: Dan first took an apprenticeship in Munich, Germany, followed by a job building and working at a brewpub in Missoula, Montana. Then they headed off to a town south of Portland, Oregon, so he could work with J.V. Northwest, an equipment manufacturing company, and finally to Anheuser-Busch, where Dan was brewing supervisor until he quit in 1993.

Dan was talented, and as he and Deb moved from one place to the next, the companies he worked for benefited, but the windfall fell just short of the Careys. They were ready to strike out their own.

Working for Themselves

Deb and Dan started their brewery with very little money and everything they had: $40,000, which came from remodeling and selling the homes they had lived in. "There was no, 'If it falls through you can come and live in our basement' from our parents," Deb says. "If it failed, we would be living in our cars."

They got a book from the bookstore on how to write a business plan. Deb did a study on demographics and why she thought breweries would work or not work in certain cities. And then they chose a place on the map. They thought Portland was saturated already with 20 breweries, although in retrospect, Deb says, they could have

settled in Oregon. They were living in Boulder at the time, but New Belgium had just opened. Deb was from Madison, and they decided to look at the Fox Valley in Wisconsin.

Deb sent Dan on a scouting trip of towns within a 30-mile radius of Madison. He discovered New Glarus, along with a 100-by-100 foot warehouse that was for sale. They moved one last time and started putting together the pieces to make their brewery; the Careys brewed their first batch of beer in 1994.

Deb Carey and her husband Dan built New Glarus
with hard work, innovation, and persistence.

Innovation

In the early years, before sales were rapidly increasing and $20 million expansions
were a possibility, Deb and Dan survived on innovative solutions for financial challenges. (That Dan was making really good beer also helped.)

When they had no money to do four-color six-packs, Deb had the idea to flip the
six-packs inside-out to reveal the natural brown color, creating a more striking look
when printing with a single color. Even though Deb is now able to afford to use more
colors or foil on her bottles, she has limited label designs to one or two signature
colors—a look distinct to New Glarus packaging: beauty in simplicity.

Deb is an accomplished artist and has designed the logos and all of the label art.
She also writes the stories that appear on the labels, now a common trend but at the
time a new idea. The thumbprint logo in the shape of Wisconsin that is imprinted on
many of the bottle caps came to Deb between brewery tours one Saturday. In a few
quiet moments, she made a print of her thumb, blew it up on a copy machine, and used
correction fluid to create the shape of Wisconsin.

Another example of Deb's ingenuity: to save the cost of making the expensive
individual tap handles for each beer, she developed a system using standard tap knobs
with magnetized tops to easily switch out the names of the beers. Small and big breweries have since followed suit and started using magnetized tap handles.

Over the years Deb has faced her share of dissenters, but sticking to her instincts has proven fruitful.

Take Spotted Cow, for instance. Deb says her distributors thought she was nuts to put a beer on the taps called Spotted Cow: Who was going to order a Spotted Cow? Although she didn't show doubt, she recalls, "In my mind I was panicking—it was either going to be a big hit or a major flop." Today Spotted Cow is New Glarus's bestseller.

Being the first woman to found a brewery has come with its share of challenges. Everyone wants to talk to Dan, she says, because "he makes all the decisions"; the idea of a female president of a brewery has been hard for many to swallow, especially when they started. But she didn't back down—and still doesn't, whether she is negotiating with banks or with wholesalers.

In a State of Constant Expansion

In its first year, New Glarus produced 3,000 barrels. The business continued to grow, and by 1997, just a few years after it had opened, space was maxed out and an expansion was needed. The hobbled-together farm equipment they were brewing with also needed upgrading. Deb and Dan took a trip to Germany in search of replacements, but the equipment at the dozen-plus breweries they visited was in horrific disrepair. "Everything was dented, or they were selling just the copper and nothing else and they wanted $200,000 for it," Deb says. It wasn't going well, until they heard about a brewery in Selb selling its equipment.

They discovered a beautiful copper brewhouse in pristine condition, dusted and shined and maintained by a man who had been running a brewery but was too disabled to run it any longer. Deb and Dan showed up the week before the scrap dealer was scheduled to come. "The man was so happy that his beloved brewhouse was going to get a new life that he sold it to us for the price of scrap metal: $27,000," Deb says.

Form meets function at New Glarus with its shiny copper brewhouse, miles of stainless steel pipes, and towering fermenters.

The catch was that they had 30 days to get it out, and they had to do it themselves. Dan stayed, hired some helpers, and went to work jackhammering out the equipment. He built crates with scrap lumber, and shipped everything to New Glarus before the 30 days had passed.

In summer 2005 Dan was installing a piece of equipment—the last component of a years-long construction project—when Deb met with her sales team, who told her sales were up 75 percent. It was only June. The news wasn't good news: there was no more room, and they had no idea what to do. Sales up 75 percent in June 2005 meant that by June 2006 New Glarus would be out of beer.

"If you let a bar owner run out of beer on a Friday, that is not a forgivable sin," Deb says. "What were we going to do?"

She and Dan started looking for land. Deb was getting nowhere and the panic was rising when she heard about a development for a Swiss community up in the hills above town. The new development fell through and the land had been sold. After a good deal of drama, Deb was finally able to buy enough land to build the Hilltop Brewery. Dan designed the equipment, Deb designed the exterior and the floor plans, and they broke ground in May 2006. They brewed their first batch in fall 2007—on the same day their first granddaughter was born.

Success

A lot of people ask why New Glarus doesn't distribute out of state. "We are growing as fast as we can in our current markets," Deb says. "If we supplied any other states, it would be an entirely different beer and entirely different company." In 2012 New Glarus produced 126,000 barrels, all distributed exclusively to Wisconsin, and it had another multimillion dollar expansion underway. It's a model that many craft brewers look up to, and considering its small beginnings, the current production and brewery campus is even more impressive.

"I think you have to have passion and a certain level of fear to be successful," Deb says. "When you start a business and you're not having nightmares in the middle of the night, then you're doing something wrong." Passion and fear might have pushed them, but Deb and Dan were determined to stick it out and willing to work their fingers to the bone to build New Glarus. They have always stayed intimately involved in the business, and still today you can find them on the brewery floor.

Dan designs all of the equipment, hunts down the ingredients, goes to Europe for hop harvest, and makes all the recipes: "I'm really proud of him; he has a gift," Deb says. "Who makes fruit beers and sours and stouts and ales and wins awards for all of them?"

In 2006 Dan won the Russell Schehrer Award for Innovation in Craft Brewing, an award given by the Brewers Association. Other recipients have included brewers from breweries including Anchor, Brooklyn Brewery, Oregon Brewing Company/ Rogue Ales, Firestone Walker, and Russian River Brewing Company.

If Dan's gift was to do the brewing and building of equipment, Deb's gift was doing everything else. She planned to run the brewery for a couple of years and then find someone to take over. "This is our 20th anniversary," she says, laughing. "That didn't really work out."

Deb says she had always planned to return to her work as an artist, but the brewery took over. In the beginning, artist friends didn't understand, telling her she was wasting her talent. But Deb says giving back to the community by creating jobs in a small town is her service. "It's a great honor to be able to participate in people's lives—to change the trajectory of their lives and their children's lives," she says. "That's what gets me up in the morning."

Deb has been able to share her success story with other small business owners and aspiring owners. She has been a member of the White House's small business council and in fall 2012, she was one of 15 small business owners invited to speak with President Obama and Vice President Biden about small business. (Of course, the president sent Deb home with some of his White House beers, made in the White House kitchen with a homebrew kit he had bought the year before.)

"To be successful at business you have to have a passion for something that you want to do that is bigger than yourself," Deb says. "For us it was the idea of making world-class beer for our friends in Wisconsin. That has been our goal: it's what we do, and it is our mission statement that always kept us focused."

THREE FLOYDS BREWING COMPANY

MUNSTER, INDIANA

Everything about Three Floyds is intense. First, the beer itself: aggressive, in-your-face flavors with ABVs that often hit double digits. Then, the label art: wild and green-faced characters, nefarious-looking kings and jokers, a red-eyed and fang-baring wolf, angry skulls—images that might haunt you in your sleep. And finally, the brewery's cult followers, who are sure to get that six-pack of just-bottled Zombie Dust before you, to snatch Dark Lord Day tickets before your page has even loaded, and to make it to the front of any line that forms outside of the little brewery in Munster, Indiana.

Then you meet Nick Floyd. A soft-spoken, humble guy who seems a little surprised that the business he opened to make beer he likes has become what it has: one of the world's top craft breweries with a loyal—if not a little insane and a lot obsessed—flock of fans. This is Three Floyds today, but when it started in 1996, it was just a few guys who wanted to make some good beer.

Starting Small

Nick started homebrewing when he was 18. "Originally I didn't like beer because everyone was drinking warm Old Style in high school," he says. "Eventually I had some German beer, and then some West Coast craft beer, and it's been downhill from there." He smiles.

Owners
NICK FLOYD,
CHRIS BOGGESS,
BARNABY STRUVE

Brewmaster
NICK FLOYD

Head Brewer
CHRIS BOGGESS

Established
1996

Production Volume
30,000–40,000 BARRELS (2012)

Distribution
ILLINOIS
INDIANA
KENTUCKY
OHIO
WISCONSIN

Website
3floyds.com

Owners Chris Boggess (left) and Nick Floyd stop for a smile, proving it's not zombies and scary monsters all the time.

Nick studied at the Siebel Institute of Technology in Chicago, and when he was 22 he moved to Florida to take the only brewery job he could find—brewing on a huge 300-barrel system. After a year of bad equipment (cast-iron vessels from the 1940s), bad treatment, and $4-an-hour pay, he returned to Chicago to work at the Weinkeller Brewery. During the time he was there from 1993 to 1994, Nick gained experience brewing a wide range of beers—doppelbock, weissbier, pale ale—but his employer was intolerant of Nick's aspirations to one day open his own brewery. Nick quit the Weinkeller to work for Golden Prairie, one of Chicago's first (now defunct) craft breweries, whose owner didn't mind Nick's plans for the future.

In 1996 Nick opened Three Floyds in Hammond, Indiana, with his brother, Simon, and his dad, Michael. With their limited budget of $50,000, Hammond's rental prices made more sense than Chicago's. It was a slow start. "It was brutal," Nick says. "We were making hoppy stuff like Alpha King and a lot of people in the Midwest weren't ready for that kind of hoppiness."

Three Floyds started with eight Chicago draft accounts and grew from there. Alpha King was the brewery's first beer, followed by Pride & Joy, Robert the Bruce, and Behemoth—all beers they still make today. From the beginning, the Floyds have had a consistent objective: to try to make the best beer possible, according to their personal taste as brewers, instead of brewing to meet a specific style. "We brew it because we like it," Nick says. "If someone buys it, then great. That was our original way of doing things."

Over time people did start to buy it. Drinkers became accustomed to hoppier, more alcoholic beers. The '90s were tough, but Three Floyds developed a core market that consistently gave positive write-ups and high ratings online—its "silent salesmen."

But it wasn't until 2002—when Three Floyds moved to its current facility in Munster, Indiana, opened a brew-pub, and started bottling its own beer—that things took off. Before the move it contract-bottled at August Schell's and Dubuque breweries, which would brew and bottle the beer at their facilities, a practice commonly employed by new breweries just getting off their feet. Nick says the beer was good but not the same as what he and his brewers were making on their own turf.

Get a Pint

KUMA'S CORNER
Chicago, Illinois
kumascorner.com
••••
THE MAP ROOM
Chicago, Illinois
maproom.com
••••
HOPLEAF
Chicago, Illinois
hopleaf.com
••••
RIDGEWOOD TAP
Homewood, Illinois
••••
BONE DRY
Highland, Indiana

When Three Floyds started its own bottling, the brewery reined in its distribution area from the East Coast and throughout the Midwest to focus on Indiana and Illinois. In 2012 production was around 30,000 barrels a year, heading to 40,000. "Even now it's hard to make enough beer for the local market," Nick says. "We'd probably be in 50 states if we had a bigger brewery." Nick says some retailers, unaware of Three Floyds' size, get upset when they are limited to one case a week.

The brewery might not make a lot of beer, but Three Floyds brewers do make a lot of *kinds* of beer. Along with the original beers, the lineup includes Gumballhead, "a refreshing American Wheat Beer that doesn't suck"; Jinx Proof, a lager; Arctic Panzer Wolf, a huge IPA with 100 IBUs (International Bittering Units) and 9.5 percent ABV; Dreadnaught, an intensely hoppy imperial IPA; and Zombie Dust, an aromatic pale ale that smells as good as it tastes. Three Floyds barrel-ages beers at its pub regularly: every month it releases a different 22-ounce seasonal beer, which might change from year to year. Trying to remember all of the monthly releases and one-offs, Nick laughs, "It's hard to keep track."

Zombie Dust is a year-round beer, but it's hard to keep the hop in constant supply, so production varies greatly month-to-month. "We have to keep changing hops we use, and we don't really name the hops we use because then they become very scarce," Nick says with a laugh. "That hop was Citra; any good brewer knows it's an awesome hop."

When Three Floyds released Gumballhead, everyone wanted to know the hop. It was Amarillo, and once word got out it became hard to get. Nick says they now rely on three-year hop contracts in order to keep brewing beer with specialty hops.

Dark Lord Day

Three Floyds had never brewed a Russian stout, and the brewers at nearby Flossmoor Brewing kept winning medals for theirs. Nick and his brewers figured they could make one just as good, if not better. In 2003 they made a strong Russian stout (it had an ABV of 13 percent) brewed with coffee and called it Dark Lord. They sold the first batch draft-only at the pub through the to-go window kiosk, and soon it was all over the Internet, heralded as one of the best beers around.

The first official Dark Lord Day was in 2004, when the brewers first bottled it. There was a line of 10 people outside the brewery waiting to buy it—a big crowd for a Thursday. When Three Floyds released the 2005 bottles—a single pallet of beer—Nick and his crew were surprised by the 100 or so people who showed up outside. The brewery limited sales to four bottles per person and sold out in one night. "We thought, 'Wow, next year we have to make double,'" Nick says. In 2006 thousands descended. That's when it turned into "a veritable circus" of tents, food, and bands.

A day in the life at Three Floyds: bottling, packaging, and a pallet of Zombie Dust.

Three years ago, the brewery started selling tickets, largely to control crowds. The area was being crowded by the thousands who came to this one tiny spot, stopping traffic and creating chaos along the way.

Every year the event gets bigger and tickets sales grow. In 2012 Three Floyds sold 6,000 tickets. In 2013 they increased ticket sales, raised prices (from $20 to $30), and expanded capacity by using a park down the road from the brewery.

Three Floyds calls the tickets "golden tickets," and while you don't have to eat through a chocolate candy bar to get one, they're nearly as hard to come by as Wonka's were—they're sold online and gone in an instant.

When tickets first went for sale, locals gave the brewery grief for selling them only online. The next year Three Floyds offered 1,000 tickets for sale directly from the brewpub. Within an hour of sales, however, tickets were on StubHub, selling for three or four times face value.

Dark Lord Day spawns a lot of dark behavior, beyond simple scalping. Nick says some offenders have executed perfect forgeries of the tickets. Forging the ticket isn't as easy as it might sound. There is a scratch-off component, which relates to yet another layer of the Dark Lord madness: ticket-holders scrape away the surface in hopes of finding a YES, which gives them the option to buy the barrel-aged variant of Dark Lord, a style that changes every year (recent versions have included vanilla bourbon barrel–aged and chili pepper–aged cognac varieties). These rarities cost anywhere from $30 to $50 per 750 mL bottle.

One year, Nick says, there was a guy in the parking lot bottling eight-ounce bottles from the larger bottles of Dark Lord and reselling them. This might be the biggest offense of all to the Dark Lord makers. "We bottle beer sanitarily with low oxygen for a reason, because it's perishable," Nick says. "And when you do it in the parking lot and sell it as the same product, well, it's not the same product."

Nick starts to laugh a little when he talks about Dark Lord Day and all of the hype, the pursuit of the scratch-off golden tickets, and the obsession that inspires the stunts by people who want their beer—like it's a beast that is out of his hands.

No doubt, Dark Lord Day has its share of Veruca Salts and Augustus Gloops.

There are also drinkers who simply love Three Floyds and the day itself. They come for the chance to taste Dark Lord, to mingle with other beer cognoscenti, to listen to music, and to taste beers from all over the country and the world. Although Nick says they don't exactly condone it, beer trading is a big part of Dark Lord Day. West Coasters come to trade bottles with East Coasters, and shared tastings start first thing in the morning before the gates open.

It's a day that brings with it a lot of fanatic behavior, outsider criticism, and general chatter, but one simple thing is true: Dark Lord Day would not be a beer drinker's cross-country pilgrimage and a bottle of Dark Lord wouldn't resell in the upper hundreds if the beer itself weren't really, really good.

The Company of Others

When Three Floyds opened a brewpub, the owners had the genius money-raising idea to put the business plan online, offering a share of the pub and a pint a day for $500. They raised half of the money through online supporters and pieced together the rest.

Bottles of Dark Lord are
sealed with red wax.

A few years ago Mike Sheerin, a 2010 *Food & Wine* Best New Chef and former chef de cuisine at Chicago's Michelin-starred restaurant Blackbird, was between gigs when he came on as chef at the Three Floyds brewpub. When Mike left to open his own restaurant in Chicago, Edward Lee, a lauded Louisville chef, started helping Three Floyds with its menu. "In the beginning we had tater tots. Now I like to think the food is on par with the beer," Nick says. "We actually get write-ups for food now, which is pretty cool."

Three Floyds brewers know how to attract and keep good company; collaborations have included beer made with Dogfish Head Brewery in Maryland as well as with Piece, Half Acre, and Revolution in Chicago. They have made beers with metal bands, including Pig Destroyer, Iron Fire, and the Chicago band Lair of the Minotaur, and they have also created a series of barley wines using different grains with Mikkeller in Denmark.

Three Floyds has also made beer with BrewDog, a Scottish craft beer company. "We went to Scotland and learned all kinds of different things," Nick says. "The more you travel and talk to other breweries, the more you learn. If you talk to the same ten breweries in Chicago you're not going to gain much extra knowledge, but you go to Scotland or England or Germany or Denmark, you'll learn a lot, and they learn from you."

Soon Munster, Indiana, won't be the only Three Floyds mecca; plans to open a pub in Chicago are underway, and Nick has also mentioned the idea of opening a place in Western Europe with Mikkeller's Mikkel Borg Bjergsø.

How do you say *Dark Lord* in Dutch?

TWO BROTHERS BREWING COMPANY

WARRENVILLE, ILLINOIS

Jason Ebel had only been in Paris for a couple of days when a few Parisians he had just met invited him to a sidewalk café for a beer. Like most American 20-year-olds in the early '90s, he was only familiar with the big-name US beers he could get his hands on easily. He didn't recognize the café beers, so his new friends suggested a raspberry one from Belgium. "I thought, 'Wow, they can put raspberries in beer? That's pretty weird,'" Jason says. "I tried it and it was sweet and sour and fruity all at the same time, and it blew me away."

He got on a train that weekend and went to Belgium to try more of what he had tasted in Paris: lambics.

Arriving in Brussels, he found a bar off the Grand Place, walked in and asked the man behind the bar for his most authentic lambic. The man took one look at him, said nothing, and poured a glass of milky, straw-colored liquid that looked nothing like the pink fruity stuff Jason had loved at the café. The man set down a plate of sugar cubes next to the glass and stood, arms crossed, watching Jason as he drank it. "I took a sip and thought I was going to vomit, it was so sour, with no fruit," Jason says. "I drank the whole thing, with no sugar, and walked out of the bar." He laughs, "I said, I learned two things: One, I will never do that again; and two, if that is beer, and the fruity

Owners
JIM AND JASON EBEL

Brewmaster
JASON EBEL

Established
1996

Production Volume
32,000 BARRELS (2012)

Distribution
FLORIDA
ILLINOIS
INDIANA
MINNESOTA
NEW YORK
OHIO
PENNSYLVANIA (SOON)

Website
twobrosbrew.com

thing I had in Paris was beer, and Budweiser and Miller is beer, then I gotta find out more about this." Jason spent the next year of his study-abroad program traveling across Europe, trying as much beer as he could.

Two Brothers

Back home in Naperville, Illinois, Jason's brother, Jim, had been homebrewing from a homebrew kit his girlfriend had given him for his birthday. When he returned from France, Jason told Jim about the beers he had tasted, Jim told Jason about the beers he had made, and they shared their ideas and started brewing together in Jim's kitchen.

The brothers opened a homebrew store in Naperville to sell supplies locally. They ran the store while Jim went to law school and Jason pursued a career in architecture. But the desire to brew kept pulling at Jason.

Jason left his architecture career and went to school for brewing, and the brothers started gathering money and equipment. With their parents, they put everything on the line to open the brewery, including their houses and cars. They converted old milk and cream tanks into fermenters and began to piece together their brewery.

Early in 1997, they brewed the first batch of beer using an incredibly manual system. They milled into 55-gallon garbage cans, which they had to haul up to the brewhouse to mash in. On his way to law school in the morning, Jim would stop by to help Jason manually dump the couple hundred pounds of grain, and then he'd return to the brewery after school to help out.

"It was a labor of love," Jason says, remembering how frugally he and his wife lived for years in order to support the brewery. "Those days were tough. If I wasn't so stupid or so stubborn I would have quit a hundred times by now. But we did it for the passion, not for the money."

In their first year of business, they brewed 164 barrels. They had two fermenters, and during the couple of weeks it took to brew their beer, Jason would go into the city with half-gallon growlers to try to get accounts. The Chicago craft beer environment was drastically different from today, and the landscape was barren.

The bottling line (which was recently replaced with a larger system); Weyermann malt from Bamberg, Germany; Long Haul ready for distribution.

Get a Pint

BIGBY'S POUR HOUSE
Addison, Illinois
••••
PINSTRIPES
Oak Brook, Illinois
pinstripes.com
••••
BAVARIAN LODGE
Lisle, Illinois
bavarian-lodge.com
••••
FOUNTAINHEAD
Chicago, Illinois
fountainheadchicago.com

"I hadn't yet gotten my first account," Jason says, "and there was a bar with a sign out front advertising a bunch of different beers. I went in and said to the manager that we were a new craft brewery and asked if he would try our beers." The manager said sure, put down three rocks glasses, and told Jason to pour the three beers he had brought. The manager threw one back after another and then said, "Nope, didn't like them." Jason got in his car, devastated; he had put so much into those beers. "I look at that compared to now and the places who now come to us, asking to carry our beer. We've come a long way," Jason says.

Two Brothers' production volume was around 32,000 barrels in 2012. When Jim and Jason started, their goal was 30,000 barrels a year, and they have been in a constant state of expansion ever since. To keep the beer close and meet their current demand, they distribute to six states.

"Our goal is not to take over the world, or even every state in the Midwest," Jason says. "Our goal is to be a great Chicago-area brewery that happens to distribute a little outside of this market."

The Beers

Two Brothers is known for making European styles of beer you don't commonly see on taps and stocked on shelves. The first beer Two Brothers produced was Ebel Weiss. Jason says a good German wheat beer is one of the harder beers to make, and they designed their first brewhouse so that they would be able to make it on a regular basis. (Their brewery became one of the first to brew a hefeweizen year-round, whereas most tend to release it as a seasonal summer beer.)

A hefeweizen also takes a much longer time to brew. Jason says while they can make a pale ale in six hours, a hefeweizen takes ten. It has paid off: Ebel Weiss won the silver at Great American Beer Festival, and the *New York Times* called it the best hefeweizen made in the United States.

At the beginning, Jim and Jason, wanting to set themselves apart, created a collection of beers that didn't include a pale ale. It took six years before their distributors wore them down to include a pale ale in their lineup to offer to wholesalers.

They named their pale ale The Bitter End, a nautical term that means the end of your rope—they'd held on to the bitter end before finally giving in to pale ale demand.

More in line with their brewing style is their flagship beer Domaine DuPage, a French-style country ale. "There is an indigenous style of beer in rural northern France and southern Belgium in an area traditionally called Brabant, which is home to communal breweries in small areas where anybody can come and brew," Jason says. "It's like they all got together 2,000 years ago and said, 'Here's the recipe'—they all brew the same one."

Jason brought the recipe home, and Two Brothers brewed the ale for a local French restaurant. Drinkers loved it, Two Brothers bottled it for the 222nd anniversary of Bastille Day, and soon it became a flagship.

Every year Two Brothers releases a holiday beer called Bear Tree. It's a wheat wine—with an ABV around 12 percent, the brewery is required by law to call it wine—and every year the name and the recipe stay the same, but everything else changes.

"All the raw ingredients we get weekly are different, so to keep a recipe consistent, we have to get a malt analysis, a hop analysis, and we are constantly tweaking recipes a little bit," Jason says. "Big brewers blend and blend and blend so you can never taste a difference. With us we brew it, put it in packaging, and hope it's close to the last one."

But with Bear Tree, they decided to see what mother nature does with the raw ingredients, so they kept the recipe the same, without any tweaking. Every year the beer varies wildly.

In early 2013 the brothers collaborated with Stone Brewery in California to brew a coffee IPA. Two Brothers had just started roasting their own coffee, 800 pounds of which were used to brew an unusual coffee beer, hoppy and light in color.

Beyond Beer

Coffee is the brewery's latest addition to its many endeavors, which include two restaurants and plans for a new café. Sourcing from coffee growers with organic and sustainable practices, Jason says he and Jim know their farmers well and deal directly with them through two programs that connect buyers to farmers: Crop to Cup and Thrive.

Food has played an important role for the brothers from the beginning, and food-friendly beer has always been a priority. "When we were in Europe, we saw how beer and wine really brought people together," Jason says. He encourages people to stay for a while at their restaurants, come together with friends and family, take a moment to slow down, and enjoy themselves—and tries to take his own advice.

"The main thing to remember when it comes to craft brewing is to have fun," Jason says. "This is a business, but you still gotta have fun and you have to get back to why you started."

Jason says he isn't surprised by the explosion of craft breweries in the Midwest. "The craft beer community is the coolest to be a part of: everyone is friendly, we share knowledge, and it revolves around something that is really fun to do," he says. "And it's tangible. At the end of the day you can go and drink what you made."

BREWER'S PLAYLIST

RUSTED ROOT • Send Me on My Way
LED ZEPPELIN • Kashmir
JOSEPH ARTHUR • Tattoo
THE LUMINEERS • Flowers in Your Hair
THE HOOTEN HALLERS • She Used to Love My Music
CELTIC FROST • Nocturnal
GG ALLIN & THE JABBERS • Cheri Love Affair
RAW POWER • Fuck Authority
RKL • Evil In You
DEVO • Smart Patrol/Mr. DNA
GRATEFUL DEAD • Anything
AMY WINEHOUSE • Valerie
BEASTIE BOYS • Sure Shot
YONDER MOUNTAIN STRING BAND • Holding
RAGE AGAINST THE MACHINE • Wake Up

FOUNDERS BREWING COMPANY

GRAND RAPIDS, MICHIGAN

ave Engbers remembers the first time he ever tried craft beer. He was 16 years old and visiting his older brother in California, when he had a Mendocino Red Tail Ale. "I joke that it was the sip that changed my life," Dave says. "But it really was—all of a sudden it opened up a whole new world to me." When he was 19, Dave's parents bought him his first homebrew kit.

Dave Engbers and Mike Stevens were both born and raised in Grand Rapids, Michigan, and they both attended Hope College in Holland, Michigan, where they met. They worked for beer wholesalers in college—a good way to get beer inexpensively—but their interest in beer went beyond that of most college kids. As graduation neared, they started looking at the brewing industry, and it became a dream to start their own brewery.

After graduation, Mike worked for his dad's company and Dave was an elementary school teacher. But the pipe dream wasn't gone; Mike had started a business plan, and Dave was still homebrewing every weekend. "It got to the point where either we were going to do this or not," Dave says. "I called Mike and said that I never want to say, 'What if?'" If it worked, great; if it didn't, they were young enough to bounce back and do something new.

It turned out that for the first four years, it didn't work.

Founders
MIKE STEVENS, DAVE ENGBERS

Brewmaster
JEREMY KOSMICKI

Established
1997

Production Volume
71,000 BARRELS (2012);
130,000 BARRELS (2013)

Distribution
ALABAMA / CONNECTICUT
FLORIDA / GEORGIA
ILLINOIS / INDIANA
IOWA / KENTUCKY
MAINE / MASSACHUSETTS
MICHIGAN / MINNESOTA
MISSOURI / NEW HAMPSHIRE
NEW JERSEY / NEW YORK
NORTH CAROLINA / OHIO
PENNSYLVANIA / RHODE ISLAND
SOUTH CAROLINA / TEXAS
VERMONT / VIRGINIA
WISCONSIN

Website
foundersbrewing.com

Brewmaster Jeremy Kosmicki (left), Dave Engbers, and Mike Stevens (right) share a pint in the taproom.

Failing

Three years after Mike and Dave had started the brewery, they had the federal government, the local bank, and their landlord after them for a total combined debt of more than a million dollars. They were drowning in the business of the brewery they had opened in 1997, and they were considering bankruptcy.

They had been running from the problem for a year, throwing money where and when they could. They owed the federal government more than $500,000 in beer excise taxes, and they had defaulted on their $500,000 bank loan. Things came to a head when the landlord called and gave them a week to come up with the money owed, or he would chain and padlock the building and shut down the business.

It wasn't as simple as trying to figure out how to pay the landlord. They first had to find a way to pay the $500,000 they owed the bank, because the only way to pay the landlord was to get investors to help, but investors wouldn't help if the bank was foreclosing on the business. All of the pieces of the puzzle had to be figured out in a week.

Mike approached one of their investors with their story and need for half a million dollars. The investor had inspirational words of wisdom to offer, but not much else. Mike left the meeting with the weight of impending doom.

But a few days later the bank called and told them they were off the hook: the investor had personally guaranteed the loan, allowing them to restructure. From there, additional investors helped with the landlord fees. And Founders was back on its feet, albeit unsteadily.

"It gave us the fire and the ability to say, 'This isn't fun anymore; why are we brewing all of these balanced but unremarkable beers that we don't care for?'" Dave says. Today Founders is Michigan's second largest beer maker, after Bell's, and is regarded as one of the best breweries in the country.

With 72 percent annual growth, Founders keeps up with demand with constant expansion and larger equipment.

Balanced, Unremarkable Beers

"We grew up in a time when you had to really push your product and beg distributors to buy your beer," Mike says. They had estimated that production would be 2,500 barrels the first year. Instead, it was 400. In the first years Founders was open, the business lost significant amounts of money every year: hundreds of thousands of dollars.

After they were bailed out and given their second chance in 2000, Mike and Dave took a fresh look at what they had been doing, and what had gone wrong.

"When we started we were really a copycat," Mike says. In order not to fail again, Founders had to find a way to differentiate itself.

"We were sitting with all of our beers in front of us and realized they weren't great," Mike says. "We needed to remove the ones we were making and reinvent our whole brand." From then on there was no more wheat, no more amber, and out came

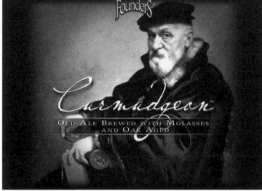

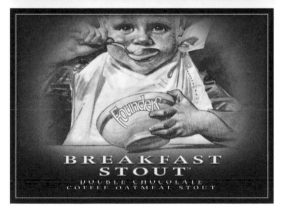

Dirty Bastard and Curmudgeon and the Breakfast Stouts.

Mike and Dave hired two new brewers and made every beer bigger and bolder, and, most importantly, made beer that they liked to drink. As soon as they saw success with the release of Dirty Bastard, they wiped the entire slate clean and reformulated every recipe.

Beer Advocate started talking about them, and word quickly spread that they were not the same brewery they had been.

Extreme Beer Fest 2004

A defining moment came in 2004 when Founders was invited to participate in the second annual Extreme Beer Fest in Boston, hosted by Beer Advocate. Founders was one of 25 breweries invited, along with breweries Dave and Mike had long-admired, including Stone, Dogfish Head, Allagash.

"We figured *extreme* beer fest," Mike says, "we better bring eight or ten of our crazy, really over-the-top beers." When they showed up, all of the other breweries had brought one or two of their main flagship beers, and nothing else. When the doors opened, hordes swarmed around the Founders booth. Dave and Mike had so many beers that they had to do timed tappings, switching to a new beer every hour.

People were waiting in line for half an hour to get one sample, only to return to the end of the line right away for the next one. "The line went clear across the whole auditorium and everyone was looking across the room asking, 'Who the hell are these guys?'" Dave says.

Tap pulls at the Founders taproom; craft beer shout-outs on a set of doors at the brewery.

At the end of the festival, the owners of the breweries they so highly admired came up to Mike and Dave and told them it was amazing what they'd done, shook their hands, and told them they had changed the dynamic of the festival forever.

"We got back in the truck tired and hungover and drove home," Mike says, "but we drove home with smiles on our faces. It made us realize there is a big play here, and we can be leaders at the table."

72 Percent Annual Growth

Although Dave and Mike had recovered the brewery in 2000 and the change in direction had proven successful, it wasn't until 2008 when they were out of the red and into the black—the same year they moved to their current production facility. Before the move, production was capped at 5,000 barrels. The first year, they produced just under 10,000. And the rapid annual growth didn't stop for the next five years; production was projected for 135,000 in 2013. "It's our responsibility to continue to

Founders' Centennial IPA makes its way
through the bottling line.

grow and to fill the need," says Dave, adding that he doesn't intend to slow production. "We want to grow aggressively but responsibly."

As demand has been increasing relentlessly, Founders has been in a constant state of physical expansion. At the start of 2013 the brewery was adding a third cellar with room to hold 32 new 500-barrel tanks. The 330- and 440-barrel tanks in the brewery's second cellar were so close to each other that they were practically touching.

Midway through 2013 Founders started brewing on a three-vessel 85-barrel brewhouse and were expecting another brew kettle and a second mash/lauter tun that were on the way. The original 30-barrel brewhouse Dave and Mike started with is still in use daily—mainly for taproom beers and test batches.

The taproom has served as a place to experiment, a playground to try out new beers and get feedback. Mike and Dave say they are constantly innovating, and they take pride in a wide range of well-crafted beers. There isn't a Founders flagship, and by not hanging their hat on one brand, they say, they can be more flexible with retailers, wholesalers, and consumers. Some people know them as the Breakfast Stout brewers, others know them as the Dirty Bastard brewers, and still others, as the Centennial IPA brewers.

"There is depth in the quality of the beers we make," Mike says. "You can buy any one of them and you're gonna make a good purchase. To me, that is what defines Founders: the brewery you can trust."

BREWER'S PLAYLIST

BLACK SABBATH
• Into the Void

10CC
• I'm Mandy Fly Me

FOUR TOPS
• Bernadette

QUEENS OF THE STONE AGE
• Feel Good Hit of the Summer

HANK WILLIAMS
• I'll Never Get Out of This World Alive

LIONEL RITCHIE
• Running with the Night

RICK JAMES
• Give It to Me Baby

ROLLING STONES
• Rocks Off

STEELY DAN
• Glamour Profession

MARTHA AND THE VANDELLAS
• Nowhere to Run

SAM AND DAVE
• Hold On, I'm Comin'

PRINCE & THE REVOLUTION
• Paisley Park

HALL & OATES
• Had I Known You Better Then

FUNKADELIC
• Get Off Your Ass and Jam

CENTRAL WATERS BREWING COMPANY

AMHERST, WISCONSIN

On January 26, 2013, Central Waters Brewing Company celebrated its 15th anniversary with a party and the limited release of its anniversary beer Fifteen. It wasn't the first anniversary beer; 1414, a barrel-aged imperial stout, was released in 1,000 barrels the year before. The new beer, Fifteen, was the same imperial stout, bourbon barrel–aged for an additional year, for a total of 26 months.

With the release of 1414, a couple of hundred people showed up. When the beer was a phenomenal success and word spread, the next year people came from far and wide to Amherst, Wisconsin—a town of just more than 1,000 people—for the release of 1,000 bottles of Fifteen. Attendees outnumbered bottles, and many who waited in line left empty-handed.

The pursuit of rare and limited-release beers is a more recent trend in the world of craft beer—Surly's Darkness, Three Floyds' Dark Lord—and the supply rarely meets the demand.

Brewers and owners like Central Waters' Paul Graham and Anello Mollica aren't trying to short the market. Instead, they're in a constant race to keep up with demand, expanding barrel capacity and continuing to put infinite amounts of planning, time, and energy into their special, barrel-aged beers that often take years to craft.

Owners
PAUL GRAHAM,
ANELLO MOLLICA

Brewmaster
PAUL GRAHAM

Established
1998

Production Volume
10,000 BARRELS (2012)

Distribution
ILLINOIS
MINNESOTA
WISCONSIN

Website
centralwaters.com

The Beginning

The original owners of Central Waters started the brewery in Junction City, Wisconsin, in January 1998. Paul had just graduated from the University of Wisconsin, where he had been homebrewing, when Central Waters brought him on to brew for the company. The owners, who had started the brewery with $40,000, were hesitant to go into debt in order to expand the business, which was failing. At the beginning of 2000, Paul bought the brewery from the owners and began to turn it around.

He increased sales, upgraded equipment, and hired more employees. When Paul took over, the brewery was producing 400 barrels a year. In 2012 they were at 8,000 barrels a year, and at the beginning of 2013, the brewery was adding fermenters to expand capacity to 14,000.

Paul and Anello met in college. Anello worked with Paul and the original owners initially but went on to work at other breweries, before he returned a few years later as part owner—once Paul had taken ownership.

Late in 2006 Central Waters built a production facility in Amherst and started producing beer there the next year. Paul also added a taproom, open on Friday and Saturday nights, to feature brewery exclusives on 12 taps.

Mudpuppy Porter leads the brewery's six flagships as the number-one seller. The brewery also releases three seasonals every year—Belgian Blonde Ale, Octoberfest Lager, and Slainte Scotch Ale. Recently, Central Waters has gained recognition for its barrel-aging program.

In 2013 Central Waters was expanding to increase its barrel-aging capacity from 1,000 barrels to 1,500 barrels. "The difficult thing is you're not looking to develop a flagship," Paul says. "You're looking to develop a high-end beer, something crazy and off-the-wall, and those take years to develop."

Take Exodus, for example: a bourbon barrel–aged sour red ale. In 2011 the brewery released only 1,500 750 mL bottles, which were hand-corked by Paul. Exodus was made with Wisconsin barley from a farm down the road and Door County cherries. After the beer fermented in cherry-lined barrels for 18 months, it was bottle-fermented for another several weeks. For the second vintage, Paul doubled the batch to release in

Get a Pint

GUU'S ON MAIN
Stevens Point, Wisconsin
guusonmain.com

••••

T-DUB'S
Waupaca, Wisconsin
tdubs-pub.com

••••

THE CRUISE BAR & RESTAURANT
Waterford, Wisconsin
thecruisetichigan.com

2013. Longer-term craft beers like these often take anywhere from two to four years to create, which means Paul needs to plan far in advance in determining how much barrel space he can afford to give to the beers that are aging for multiple years.

Green Expansion

Along with expanding capacity, Paul and Anello have been making efforts to improve Central Waters' sustainability. Not only have the efforts decreased energy use in its resource-intensive endeavor, but they've also cut business costs. Radiant floor heat lets the brewers operate with the doors wide open (for loading and unloading kegs, barrels, and bottles) in the middle of winter without worrying about heat loss. "We have a 75,000-square-foot building with

Bottles on the line ready to be
filled, capped, and labeled.

24-foot ceilings that costs us about $200 a month in the wintertime to heat—that's
how much it costs to heat my house," Paul says. "It's such an efficient way to heat, in
the long run it pays for itself."

In 2009 Central Waters installed 24 solar thermal panels for 1,000 square feet of
collection space as well as a 2,500-gallon hot water storage tank. Every day Central
Waters uses around 1,500 gallons of
water, heated to 165 degrees Fahrenheit.
Before the solar hot water upgrade, that
water was heated using natural gas;
now the water is heated to around 140
degrees with solar energy and gas heats
the rest. The preheated water is used
to clean the tanks and kegs—another
resource-intensive process. It's also
used for the radiant floor heat and the
sinks throughout the building.

"It's a pretty neat system that's
super high in return on investment," Paul says. The payback period is expected to be
about seven years, with projected savings of $1.4 million during the life of the system.
"Coupled with other energy-saving measures, we were able to double production in
2009 and not see utility costs go up a penny," Paul says.

They also added a photovoltaic array of 100 solar panels to help reduce fossil fuel
consumption. Under a net-metering policy, Central Waters contributes the energy
it produces with its solar panels to the electrical grid, effectively reducing the total
energy it consumes from the grid. Paul says this system offsets the brewery's electrical
use by approximately 23 percent.

The Next Wave

Central Waters opened right after the mid-'90s bust. "There was a big bubble that
popped for specific reasons," Paul says. "A lot of people were in it thinking they were
going to get rich and they didn't care about quality, and it turned out that consumers

really did care about quality." By finding ways to save on operation costs, carving out a niche for itself in the market with long-term barreling aging, and continuing to uphold its already established name, Central Waters is preparing for the future, and what might be another craft beer fallout.

Paul says the first 10 years were a challenge, when craft beer didn't see the shelf space that it does today and was a tough sell to get into grocery and liquor stores. It was in the days of self-distribution, before the three-tier system (legally required separation between producers and wholesalers via an independent distributor), and Paul says the only thing that kept the brewery alive was being able to keep the markup that now goes to distribution companies.

Now Central Waters is riding the next big wave of craft beer, and Paul and Anello are not sure if or when it's going to crash. Right now, it's a boon for business: Paul says the tanks he bought in 2000 sell for three times what he paid for them in the late '90s, and in 2009 he sold his brewhouse for four times what he paid. Used equipment sells so fast he doesn't even need to list it.

But with a new brewery opening daily across the country, the future feels less sure. Paul and Anello have believed in slow growth from the beginning, and Paul says that their careful planning makes him more comfortable entering into a higher-risk environment—where more and more breweries are vying for the same number of taps and the same amount of shelf space.

Now the challenge is to keep up with today's craft beer drinker, who is always looking for the next new thing, the most recent release, the latest innovation, the most exclusive limited release. Keeping Central Waters' reputation as a reliable maker of quality beers is first and foremost in Paul's mind. "Mudpuppy Porter might be your favorite beer, but you're only going to buy it one out of five times," Paul says. "What

The beginnings of a winter blizzard swirling around a barrel-aging room.

keeps people coming back is a quality product they know they can come back to, because they're not going to buy it every time."

Paul and Anello have shown that they'll stand behind the quality of their beer. In spring 2012, they issued a voluntary recall of Peruvian Morning, one of their most sought-after barrel-aged beers. One barrel was contaminated and wasn't caught before it was blended in. It was a $250,000 mistake. Central Waters issued a recall and reimbursed consumers or replaced their purchase. The contaminated beer wasn't harmful, but it had an off-taste and the wrong flavor profiles.

It might seem like an expensive move for something that might not have affected many of the bottles that were released into the market, but Paul and Anello wanted to shine light on the mistake and remedy it, to keep Central Waters' reputation as a brewery known for its quality. "Quality is the number one rule of the game right now, in my opinion," Paul says. "Anything subpar is not going to make it."

DARK HORSE BREWING COMPANY

MARSHALL, MICHIGAN

I'm a chewy," says Aaron Morse. "I like to eat my beers."

It's a fitting statement for a brewer who is sweating over a hot cooktop in a tiny kitchen, toasting a couple hundred pounds of rice for a beer inspired by a 100 Grand candy bar.

The beer was the idea of Chicago's Cleetus Friedman, chef and one-time owner of the now-shuttered City Provisions deli. Aaron and Cleetus have collaborated before; their relationship first started when Cleetus invited Dark Horse to be a part of one of City Provisions' Farm Dinners.

There are logistical problems to solve for their current collaboration, like how to melt 50 pounds of chocolate without a double boiler. Aaron and Cleetus improvise with a big metal bowl and stockpot. To prep the chocolate, Aaron finds a chisel and hammer and starts hammering away pieces from the chocolate brick. In addition to the toasted rice and melted chocolate, they'll add caramel to complete the flavor profile of the candy bar.

Toasting all of the wheat and the rice turns out to take longer than planned, a laborious and hot three-hour process, but spirits are up with the inspired process of creating a new beer on the fly. Cleetus says he loves to work with Aaron, who is willing to try unusual, sometimes crazy, flavor combinations.

Owners
AARON AND KRISTINE MORSE,
BILL AND CALLY MORSE

Brewmaster
AARON MORSE

Established
2000

Production Volume
15,000 BARRELS AND GROWING
(2012)

Distribution
ILLINOIS
INDIANA
KENTUCKY
MASSACHUSETTS
MICHIGAN
MINNESOTA
NEW YORK
NORTH CAROLINA
OHIO
PENNSYLVANIA
VIRGINIA
WISCONSIN

Website
darkhorsebrewery.com

Aaron Morse toasts rice for his 100 Grand beer; the Marshall, Michigan, brewery.

"It's a true collaborative effort," Cleetus says. "I have all of these ideas, I throw them out and Aaron says what will work."

A passerby peeks his head into the tiny, toasty room. "What are we making, boys?"

"Money!" Cleetus shouts out. "One hundred grand, baby—we're making money."

From Brewpub to Brewery

Aaron was at Northern Michigan University making beer out of his dorm room when his parents bought a bar in his hometown of Marshall, Michigan, which they planned to remodel. When they told Aaron about the bar, he suggested they open a brewpub.

They opened in October 1997, and by January 1, 2000, they were closed. "It was horrible—my parents lost tons and tons and tons of money," Aaron says. He took the brewing equipment, moved to Dark Horse's current location, and started a micro-brewery—with no restaurant attached.

The brewery started out in a room that was 10 feet by 50 feet, with the equipment packed in. Aaron brewed 400 barrels the first year, starting with seven beers. When the family-run brewpub closed, Aaron and his parents had made an agreement to pay the bank back and let their partners walk away. When they reincarnated in the form of a microbrewery, the Morse family was more conservative, and they didn't take on partners. Today the brewery is a true family business: Aaron's wife quit her job to work at the brewery full time, his mom works in the office, and his dad is a truck driver.

After a decade of careful growth and expansion, production was at 15,000 barrels in 2012, with 20,000 planned for 2013. Distribution has spread to 12 states. Aaron claims in seven years, on his 45th birthday, he'll retire. It's hard to imagine Aaron, who has the relentlessly creative spirit of an artist who never stops producing new ideas, retiring from anything.

Scary Jesus Rockstar

One of the first beers that Cleetus and Aaron collaborated on was an apricot and chamomile pale ale called Scary Jesus Rockstar.

In 2010 the band Nickelback, who has an album called Dark Horse, approached Aaron about using his company's beer in its music video that was to portray, according to Aaron, the brewery's delivery truck showing up at a frat party and lots of kids at the party holding bottles of the beer. Aaron, in truth a sweet guy, had a less-than-sweet response—more or less: "This is craft beer, not frat beer, and by the way, we don't like your band." A lot of people weren't happy, and Aaron was the recipient of a good deal of hate mail.

Get a Pint

THE MACHINE SHOP
Flint, Michigan
themachineshop.info
• • • •
KALAMAZOO BEER EXCHANGE
Kalamazoo, Michigan
kalamazoobeerexchange.com
• • • •
REGGIE'S
Chicago, Illinois
reggieslive.com
• • • •
ONE EYED BETTY'S
Ferndale, Michigan
oneeyedbettys.com
• • • •
7 MONKS
Traverse City, Michigan
7monkstap.com
• • • •
HOP CAT
Grand Rapids, Michigan
hopcatgr.com
• • • •
FOUNTAINHEAD
Chicago, Illinois
fountainheadchicago.com
• • • •
CRICKET CLUB
Battle Creek, Michigan
• • • •
LOCAL OPTION
Chicago, Illinois
localoptionbier.com

The uproar subsided until the Huffington Post wrote about it again in summer 2012. The same day the story was resurrected, Cleetus and Aaron were together to brew the apricot beer. Inspired by the Nickelback story, Cleetus gave Aaron a list of potential names, all referencing Nickelback songs, and Scary Jesus Rockstar was born.

The beer turned out to be wildly popular. Another successful Cleetus–Aaron collaboration was a sarsaparilla stout with vanilla bean. Dark Horse brewed a limited amount of the beer, and did a small-run barrel-aged version. After yearlong demand for another release, Aaron says he plans to produce a large batch and release it regularly.

Wiggs, the Beer, and the Big Beard

Dark Horse's current full-time beers are Amber Ale, Boffo Brown Ale, Raspberry Ale, Black Ale, and Crooked Tree IPA. Bryan Wiggs—known as "Wiggs"—oversees production of the year-round brews and works on recipes with Aaron.

"I was a kid brewing down the street in Battle Creek—or trying to brew—when I got yelled at by Aaron's wife backstage at a concert, who was saying her husband

made much better beer than I did," says Wiggs, laughing. An unexpected start to a friendship and a job, but Wiggs, undeterred, found Dark Horse's brewery and started hanging out after work to "watch the madness."

From 2003 to 2008, when he started working at Dark Horse full time, Wiggs did an informal apprenticeship at the brewery, which he described as "partying, drinking beers, and learning from Aaron, who I was a big fan of." Even before Wiggs was

brewing at Dark Horse, Crooked Tree was his favorite beer. "It was one of those dreams come true when you find your favorite beer and a couple of years later you're making it yourself," Wiggs says.

Dark Horse's brewers are wildly adventuresome and always experimenting. For the most part, Dark Horse beers are malt-forward—"really big, in-your-face style." At the end of the day, Wiggs says, the brewers always make beers they like to drink themselves. The taproom allows them to try out some of their more experimental batches. While the brewery has 16 beers in its full-time and part-time rotation, Dark Horse has been known to have 47 different beers on tap at once.

Wiggs, whose official business-card-printed title is Head of Brewing Operations/Token Hippy, was wearing a tie-dyed T-shirt from the Michigan Rothbury music

Crooked Tree is Dark
Horse's bestseller.

festival when I first met him. Aside from his full beard, he stood out from the rest of the staff: thickly bearded death metal fans, all clad in a similar uniform of a Dark Horse tee, Carhartt or Dickies pants, and a stocking cap. Aaron, in similar garb, has the deferential title of the Big Beard.

The staff has the greatest respect for Aaron, and everyone follows his lead, which is as fast-paced as the hare's and as untiring as the tortoise's. He thrives on doing a lot at once and appears to have a hand in everything at Dark Horse. During the 100 Grand beer rice-toasting project, he's tracking down a missing FedEx package expected to deliver sarsaparilla for the stout; receiving a phone call from his seven-year-old son; and planning for an impromptu dinner for that night, in honor of—and prepared by—their chef guest, Cleetus. Stopping for a minute, Aaron squats down to send a group invite via text to his staff, he looks up and asks, "How do you spell camaraderie?" It's easy to see why everyone loves him.

The Dark Horse crew trusts Aaron's direction, which isn't entirely planned out in advance. "I'm a very do-it-as-you-go kind of guy," Aaron says. "The intent was to build a production microbrewery and sell beer in all the states that touched the Great Lakes. So we did that, and now we need to do more." Aaron says now he plans to distribute Dark Horse everywhere east of the Mississippi.

Aaron could benefit from twice as many hours in a day. In addition to running his company and brewing, he's been making plans to expand the Dark Horse campus—already home to a brewpub, a general store (homebrew supplies, merchandise, skateboards, snowboards), and a motorcycle shop—to include a creamery, a bakery, and a candy shop, where everything is made on-site. Also on the agenda: distilling.

"I always think I'm busy," Cleetus says, "and then I come here and I feel lazy."

PIECE BREWERY AND PIZZERIA

CHICAGO, ILLINOIS

Jonathan Cutler's awards have been so numerous that he can't keep track anymore. But there is one win that stands out for him. The first year he brewed a kölsch at Piece Brewery, he won a medal at the World Beer Cup. Two brewers from Cologne, Germany, won the gold and silver, and Jonathan took home the bronze. Years before he won the award, Jonathan had had one of his most memorable beer-drinking experiences of his life in Cologne, the birthplace of kölsch.

A few years before Jonathan started brewing at Piece, when he was working at Goose Island brewpub, his parents took him and his sister to Europe, "Griswold family-style." They traveled through Germany and made a stop in Cologne. Upon arrival, he had his first kölsch, a Gaffel, and thought it was one of the best beers he had ever had. Brewers had tried to make the style at Goose, Jonathan says, and they were making a really good beer, but it wasn't a kölsch—not like the one he tasted that first night in Cologne.

The next morning, he headed to Paffgen, a brewpub with a beer garden in back. "When you show up, they put down a coaster and put a hash mark for each beer ordered," he says. Jonathan ordered a couple of kölsches and some lunch. His girlfriend showed up, and they had another; then his sister and

Owner
BILL JACOBS

Head Brewer
JONATHAN CUTLER

Established
2001

Production Volume
1,800 BARRELS (2012)

Website
piecechicago.com

her boyfriend arrived—more hash marks; and then his parents—yet more hash marks. "We were sitting in this beautiful beer garden with the copper in the background, drinking beer together and talking," Jonathan says. They stayed for dinner and drank kölsches until the garden closed. "My mom still has the coaster, marked with about a hundred hash marks." Years later he made his own medal-winning version, a beer that would prove difficult to produce fast enough to keep up with demand.

The Beginning

Jonathan was in his fifth year at Southern Illinois University, putting off graduation and enjoying homebrewing a lot more than class. He and a friend were making a keg or two a week, calling up friends to come and drink their beer. "We bought as many carboys as we could—we were brewing in these stainless steel Italian 100-liter pots, so you could make one keg at a time," Jonathan says. The first craft beer boom of the early '90s was just starting, and Jonathan found out about the Siebel Institute of Technology in Chicago. When he learned that he could get a degree in brewing, it clicked that making beer might be what he wanted to do. Jonathan completed college as quickly as possible, and enrolled in Siebel.

After school, Jonathan searched for a brewery job for six or seven months, until he heard that Leinenkugel's in Milwaukee needed someone to work on the packaging line. Just to get his foot in the door, he drove an hour every day from Libertyville, Illinois, to Milwaukee to work the line. Then one day Matt Brynildson from Goose Island called him.

Jonathan worked at Goose Island for three years, during a time—1997, 1998, and 1999—when there was practically as much talent and creativity in one place as Elizabethan England: Matt Brynildson (brewmaster at Firestone Walker), Gary Nichols (quality control at Bell's Brewery), Josh Deth (manager partner at Revolution Brewing), Jim Cibak (head brewer at Revolution Brewing), and Phin DeMink (founder of Southern Tier Brewing Company). "Back then it was a really neat environment," he says. "It was a melting pot of all of these brewers who were hungry."

It was also really hard work. There wasn't a lot of money, and the brewers often worked overnight shifts: nine at night until six in the morning. "That was awful. Also

Get a Pint

PIECE BREWERY AND PIZZERIA

Chicago, Illinois
piecechicago.com

not the best idea: I was working all night in a factory, by myself, with temperatures and pressures and chemicals all around me," Jonathan says with a laugh.

Low pay, long hours, and a relatively dangerous work environment were the tradeoffs for the experience and a job at a brewery at the time when there were very few in the city of Chicago. After taking a job on the packaging line at Goose, Jonathan realized it was time to do something else; he left Goose for California and a job at Sierra Nevada Brewing Company. Jonathan wasn't even there for a full year when an opportunity brought him back to Chicago.

Piece

Bill Jacobs was opening a New Haven–style pizza place in Chicago's Wicker Park neighborhood, and he wanted it to feature its own beer. Jonathan started brewing for Piece in July 2001, when it opened. "It was a barren landscape as far as beer was [concerned] when I came here," Jonathan says. "It was Goose, Rock Bottom, and us."

Brewpubs had come and gone, but the model didn't seem to be working in Chicago. Jonathan had a lot of ideas from the beginning about what was going to make his beer stand out, but once he started, the original manager told him that it wasn't a brewpub, just a pizza place that happens to serve its own beer.

"Hearing that, I was just crushed, and I was like, oh no, what have I done?" Jonathan says. "But I said, oh well, I'm going to make the best beer I can."

The original business plan called for a beer production volume of 500 barrels a year. In the first full year, it was already at 560. The next year, that rose to 640, and then to 750, and then to 1,000. "I did 1,001 barrels by myself and then I hired Andy the next day," he says. A lot of people had wanted to come in and work with him, but Jonathan was committed to doing it himself; he wanted it to be his, and he didn't trust anyone else to touch it. That approach just about killed him.

When Andy Coleman came in, bringing prior experience at a brewpub with him, Jonathan didn't even have to say a word before Andy got out cleaning supplies and started cleaning. Jonathan was impressed. A few months later, after training Andy to his methods, Jonathan took his first vacation in five years.

Today the two make 1,800 barrels a year together in a space so tiny that it's hard to believe those numbers. They work on a seven-barrel brewhouse, and most of the fermenters they have added are double 14-barrel tanks. With four fermenters and the brewhouse crammed into a tiny room, they have stretched capacity to such a degree that it's cramped for even one person to move around. They literally stretched their serving tanks to hold 14 barrels: instead of replacing them with larger tanks, the tanks were lifted up to the ceiling and a second seven-barrel steel attachment was soldered on below.

"This is the woe-is-me part," Jonathan says, "but every other brewpub in Chicago has more room than I do." It may be woe-is-me, but it's also true. His space constraints make it even more impressive when you consider what Jonathan has been able to produce.

Even though Jonathan has added additional fermenters next door to the pizzeria, he has hit capacity at 1,800 barrels per year, and he is considering his next move. A production facility to start packaging is one option.

The Beer

As far as his beer lineup goes, Jonathan's first effort was building the seven tap lines and seeing what people liked. After he made his kölsch, he couldn't stop making it, and Piece bought a double tank that was strictly reserved for his beloved style.

As time passed, the people on the other side of the bar started to love his hoppier beers. At first it took three weeks for an IPA to go; now it takes eight days to run through a double batch.

At one point he decided to try a hefeweizen. "A friend warned me, and told me once I did it, I'd have to make it all the time," Jonathan remembers. He was right. Jonathan won a gold medal for it and found himself making hefeweizen constantly to keep patrons happy.

Finally he made a dunkelweizen. "I was like, if you don't stop drinking this wheat beer, I'm going to go nuts!" he says. "So I decided to make a dark wheat beer and see what happened." It took a month for the dunkel to hit the same sales and demand as the hefe. Now one tap is reserved for hefeweizen half the year and dunkelweizen the other half.

Most brewers can't complain if their biggest problem is having a bar full of drinkers demanding their brew year round. The only challenge that Jonathan faces for the future is whether to keep Piece as it is—a brewpub serving their local neighborhood and the city—or to take it to the next level and open a production facility. Two things are certain: the demand for Jonathan's beer is there, and his space is maxed out.

JOLLY PUMPKIN ARTISAN ALES

DEXTER, MICHIGAN

In his spare time, Ron Jeffries crafts his own longboard skateboards and surfboards, roasts his own coffee, brews kombucha, and makes recipes for a new gluten-free product line. Admittedly, there isn't a lot of time to spare; he's also the owner-brewer of Jolly Pumpkin, the award-winning brewery in Dexter, Michigan, which makes some of the best oak-aged sour beers out there.

"There are so many things that lead a person to what they enjoy doing. You find little clues along the way through your life," says Ron, whose clues started as an undergrad at the University of Michigan, where he majored in literature but took every basic science class offered. "I didn't know it at the time, but that's a good basis for becoming a good brewer because, especially at a small brewery, you become a jack-of-all-trades."

Ron likes to say he knows a little about a lot. He also knows a lot about sour beer.

Little Clues

Ron's path to becoming a brewer started in the late '80s, when he was in graduate school at the University of Michigan's School of Natural Resources and Environment. The drummer in a band he was in signed up for a beer-of-the-month club. "He got what I know now is stale beer from all over the country," Ron says, laughing. But the club meant trying a lot of unexplored beer styles, which piqued Ron's interest.

Founders
LAURIE AND RON JEFFRIES

Brewmaster
RON JEFFRIES

Established
2003

Production Volume
5,500 BARRELS (2012);
10,000 BARRELS (2013)

Distribution
MOST STATES

Website
jollypumpkin.com

One day Ron was at the house of a friend who was homebrewing his first batch of beer. "I asked a bunch of questions and he had no answers," he says. Ron went home, thought about it, called his friend the next day, and said they should open a brewery.

His friend laughed and said they didn't know anything about starting a brewery. The conversation stopped there, but Ron changed the focus of his graduate degree to focus on industrial processes at microbreweries and brewpubs as well as issues of waste and efficiency. He studied the science of brewing, but once he had exhausted the library's books on the topic, it was time to get real experience. He put his degree on hold and began to look for brewery jobs.

Jolly Pumpkin

For the next nine years, Ron spent time brewing, setting up brewpubs, learning about materials and raw ingredients, building recipes, talking about beer, training staffers about beer and food pairings, and teaching the general public about beer appreciation. Finally he felt ready. "My goal ever since that phone call to my friend was to own a brewpub," Ron says. "And now I had a great foundation for that." He finished his business plan and convinced a small bank to give him a loan to start Jolly Pumpkin. He oversaw the build-out of his brewery in record time; he started in January and was already brewing beer in May.

"We spent the next five years just trying not to go out of business, initially because we were so undercapitalized and underfunded," he says. "And because we made a couple of big strategic errors." The first was not having an on-site taproom to build loyalty, win local fans, and create some cash flow.

The second strategic error wasn't so much a mistake as a choice, which may have added to its starting struggles, but ultimately made Jolly Pumpkin what it is today: to do 100 percent oak-aged sour beer—well before anyone else was doing it.

Oak-Aged Sour Beers

When Ron first started brewing beer, the attention was on pale ales. Then it was porters and stouts. By the early 2000s IPAs and extreme beer had taken over the craft brewer's focus. "I could see there was this whole segment of beer that was unexplored

Jolly Pumpkin on draft at the Ann Arbor bar; the brewhouse at the Dexter brewery.

by American craft brewers," Ron says, "and I started to focus my business plan on doing Belgian-style aged beers." At the time Allagash in Portland, Maine, and Ommegang in Cooperstown, New York, were making them, but few others were, and Ron saw a niche that was ripe for a craft brewer with passion, drive, and skills.

The summer before Ron acquired his small business loan, relatively late in the Jolly Pumpkin planning process, he was sitting on his backyard patio with his wife, drinking an oak-aged sour beer when he said to his wife, "Wouldn't it be the best if we could just make beer like this—oak-aged sour beer?" And she said, "Why don't you?"

"The next thing you know we're doing all oak-aged sour beer," Ron says. "I thought this was an even better idea because nobody was doing this to the extent we were planning to do it, which was 100 percent."

Get a Pint

JOLLY PUMPKIN

Ann Arbor and
Traverse City, Michigan
jollypumpkin.com

• • • •

HUMPY'S

Kailua-Kona, Hawaii
humpys.com

• • • •

MALA OCEAN TAVERN

Lahaina, Hawaii
malaoceantavern.com

• • • •

HONU SEAFOOD AND PIZZA

Lahaina, Hawaii
honumaui.com

• • • •

MAUI BREWING CO.

Lahaina, Hawaii
mauibrewingco.com

Ron had some experience souring beers at breweries where he had worked in steel, buying wild yeast and lactic cultures. He wasn't very impressed with the results, which he said were one-dimensional. But he had made one oak-aged sour beer.

Ron had taken an IPA, a hefeweizen, and some cherries; mixed them together in an oak barrel; and allowed the natural wild yeast on the cherries to sour the beer. "I came out with this fantastic beer that, in the mid-to-late '90s, was really not appreciated by any of the guests at the bars," he says with a laugh. He admits to a few technical flaws—there were chunks of cherries in the beer itself, which hadn't been strained or filtered—but the beer was Ron's aha moment when he realized he needed to use wild, naturally occurring cultures, rather than store-bought.

Jolly Pumpkin started with 21 oak barrels and two large oak-aging tuns. Ron's idea was that by reusing the barrels, the natural wild yeast of the Dexter area would populate the barrels and sour the beer. "Wild yeast is everywhere in the air, and it will

show up if you give it a nice happy home to live in, like a barrel full of beer," Ron says. "We took a leap of faith that the wild yeast of Dexter could create good beer." They were fortunate that it did.

It takes awhile for yeast to grow, however, and for the first half year, the brewery didn't have sour beer. And then Jolly Pumpkin went through a shift, when its customers were enjoying a nice oak-aged beer that was slowly becoming more tart and more sour, with the distinct aroma and flavor of *Brettanomyces* yeast. "People were wondering what was going on," Ron says. "We did a lot of explaining. But we thought, this is great—nobody else is doing this and everybody is going to love it."

A lot of people did love it—the very first summer Ron's brewery won a gold medal at the Great American Beer Festival (GABF)—but it was also a hard sell because there wasn't the education about sour beer that there is today. For five years, Jolly Pumpkin struggled to sell enough to stay in business.

The gold medal at the GABF caused a lot of people to take notice of what Ron was doing. Jolly Pumpkin won award after award, and a lot of articles were written about the beer, but the brewery still struggled. "It was like, 'Great, another gold medal—but the phone bill's due,'" Ron laughs.

Slowly, things began to change. Ron's beers created a lot of curiosity in other brewers, who began brewing sours. Some breweries added entire sour programs, and beer drinkers across the country began to learn more about sour beers. "Our beer is expensive to make, and it can be pretty pricey," Ron says. "But once people had an experience with a sour beer and what it was supposed to taste like, they were more comfortable in making that purchase."

The opening of Jolly Pumpkin pubs—one on the Mission Peninsula near Traverse City and one in Ann Arbor—coupled with the spread of sours across the country caused an explosion of interest: Jolly Pumpkin doubled its sales in 2009.

The doubling continued every year until 2012, when the brewery was maxed out at its original plant on Broad Street in Dexter, Michigan. Production was 5,500 barrels at the end of 2012.

"The demand was insane for our beers," Ron says. They had a choice to scale down to a more comfortable pace or to build a bigger brewery that would meet demand.

He and his wife talked about it and remembered their original vision. At the beginning, a lot of people asked Ron how big he planned to get. "I'd laugh and say, tongue-in-cheek, 'I'll make as much sour beer as people want to drink,'" he says. In keeping with that ethos, Ron opted to expand.

Making Sours

Ron starts his beers the same way any other brewer would: mashing in, boiling the wort, adding hops, and then moving it to primary fermentation. Ron uses open fermentation (that isn't what sours the beer—there are a lot of open-fermentation breweries that don't make sour beers) and from there, everything is aged in oak, where naturally occurring wild yeast and sour cultures are present. That's an important distinction in what Ron does: he doesn't buy *Brettanomyces* or *Lactobacillus*.

Jolly Pumpkin uses the wild yeast
from the area to sour its beers.

After aging, some Jolly Pumpkin beers are packaged in batch format; Ron calls these "fresher" sours. With other beers that have been aged for longer periods of time, batches are blended. "There may be a lot of similarities, but there are a lot of differences, and those are magnified over time," Ron says. "The only way to do it is to taste the beer, create sample blends, and pick the sample blends I like the most." After he blends the beer, it goes through an additional fermentation in the bottle. The beer, unfiltered and unpasteurized, continues to develop its sourness and wild yeast–character in the bottle.

Making wild and sour beers at Jolly Pumpkin is expensive and labor intensive. Using open fermenters and emptying the barrels into packaging tanks takes more work than moving beer from one stainless steel tank to another.

For the first several years, Ron listened to the advice of wholesalers who told him he had to hit a certain price point and that if the beer cost more than that, no one would buy it. He almost went out of business. He changed his model, figured out how much the beer cost to make, and what he needed to charge in order to stay in business. The prices of Jolly Pumpkin beer doubled, and people started buying twice as much.

Ron says that in the time since Jolly Pumpkin sales started drastically increasing, the country has been experiencing a period of extreme sour beers. When he used to take his beers to shows and festivals, people always said how sour it was. Today, with the same beers—if anything, slightly more sour versions—a common response is, "That's not *that* sour."

Ron says he sees the shift turning away from big beers that are more challenging to drink and to enjoy and back to beers that make you want to have another one. In other words, what he has been doing all along. But it isn't always easy to pin down or to figure out what makes a beer so enjoyable and drinkable—and likely to make someone want another.

"It's the blending of the art with the science, and that's really where the art takes over," Ron says. "You can work all the calculations and figure out your IBUs and your extract yields, but you can't really figure out the art."

SHORT'S BREWING COMPANY

BELLAIRE AND ELK RAPIDS, MICHIGAN

F our years after Joe Short started brewing beer at his brewpub in Bellaire, Michigan, production was maxed out. Joe and his wife, Leah, were working seven days a week, 18 hours a day, brewing beer and running the pub together. Joe bussed tables and ran food, Leah cooked in the kitchen, and at the end of the day they did the books. Worn down, overworked, and with no room to expand, they realized it was do or die.

In 2008 they bought a building 30 miles away in Elk Rapids and started work on a new production facility. But halfway through construction, they were out of money. Dead in the water, they were short $200,000. Joe was straining under the pressure.

One day he was at the pub trying to fix a problem with the tap when an older man at the bar started asking him about the Mug Club. There was a long wait to join the Short's Mug Club, and Joe told him he'd have to add his name to the waiting list. The man persisted: "I'm not going to live forever, and I really want one of these mugs." Patience flagging, Joe said, "Sorry man, just like everybody else, we'll put you on the list." He escaped downstairs to work on the regulator. When Joe came back up to the bar, the patron wasn't relenting. "Come on, how much would it take for me to get a mug?"

Owners
JOE AND LEAH SHORT

Brewmaster
TONY HANSEN

Established
2004

Production Volume
8,000 BARRELS (2012);
23,000 BARRELS (2013)

Distribution
MICHIGAN

Website
shortsbrewing.com

Joe looked straight at him. "I know exactly how much it's going to take. It's going to take $200,000 for you to have a mug." And he turned to head back downstairs. But before he got to the door, the man caught up with him and said, "Ok, I'm in." Joe stared at him. "I think you have a good thing going right here," he continued. "But I'm going to give you $250,000, because I know you need it." So Jim May gave Joe a simple loan to finish production, and Joe gave Jim a mug. In January 2009, Short's brewed its first batch of beer in Elk Rapids.

The Woodmaster

The story of Jim May sounds like a story about arbitrary and incredible luck, but it's really a story about Joe. Jim wasn't the first to offer support to Joe with little more to go on than blind faith and trust in what Joe was doing.

Joe is earnest and easy to like. He is paced and intentional when he talks, but it's a pace of someone who seems never to tire. He keeps all of the specific details of past projects in his head and yet still has capacity to constantly plan for what's next. And Joe always wants to do what's next.

Joe started making beer before he could buy it—in 1998. When he was a junior at Western Michigan University, he left school to pursue brewing full time. He worked at a few breweries across Michigan, learning the craft and finding his own style, and he was at a brewpub in Jackson, Michigan, when he decided to start his own brewery. At the time he was dating a girl from his high school and was close to her family, and to her dad Bill Sohn. The last beer Joe had brewed before he left the Jackson brewery was an imperial stout. He brought two of the bottles to Bill, and they drank them together while Joe told Bill his idea for a brewery. He'd found a building in Bellaire and some equipment for sale. After drinking Joe's beer and hearing his plans, Bill told Joe to buy the equipment and sign the lease, and Bill Sohn became Joe's first lender. A woodworker by trade, he's also the inspiration for Woodmaster, the brewery's American brown ale.

Joe opened Short's in Bellaire in 2004. Working with nearly no budget, he used his ingenuity to build out the pub. Tables were crafted out of 100-year-old barn wood; there were chairs from old bus seats and windows reused from a nearby cottage. It

was a community effort to finish the pub, and volunteers were often paid in store credit (i.e., beer).

"When Short's started, it was just Joe starting with a vision and giving people his word that he would work hard and repay any loans," says Matt Drake, chief operations officer. "That led to a creativity and a spirit that has been part of our mission ever since."

The Imperial Beer Series

After Short's opened, Joe started work on a yearlong project called the Imperial Beer Series. He wanted it to be "an expression of the pinnacle of quality and creativity of the beer" that his company could make in their little brewery in Northern Michigan.

The series was 13 beers, most of which Joe had never made before. Because he didn't have money to experiment with test batches, Joe wrote recipes based on how he thought they would taste, and he had only one chance to make them. "A lot were first-time ever brews, so that said something to a lot of people about my ability to just go for it on a whim and produce a really high-quality, interesting beer," Joe says.

Joe's focus was to create a beer every month, package it, store it in the cooler, and then put together a beer dinner in the spring and present a slideshow of the project. Short's spent all the money it had made that year on the project, ordering a pallet of glass at a time, spending money as it came in. Joe, with help, hand-bottled in 750 mL bottles. Each bottle had a hang-tag that told the story of the beer: Woodmaster described Joe's relationship with Bill, for example, and the Spruce Pilsner told a story about our forefathers using spruce tips in beer. Each tag listed the yeast strain, the alcohol percentage, and the number of the bottle. Each tag was also hand-signed by Joe.

Leah designed the 13-course beer pairing dinner in their tiny kitchen. They rented glasses and tablecloths. The beer was sold in handmade wooden crates that they hand-branded. Even the brander itself was made by a friend of Joe's. It was the ultimate hand-crafted project.

The idea was to sell a lot of the beer. Although the limited edition runs weren't big—around 650 to 850 bottles per batch—Short's hardly sold any, and it took more than a year and a half to eventually sell it all.

Bottling and fermenting at
the Elk Rapids facility.

Get a Pint

THE PYRAMID SCHEME
Grand Rapids, Michigan
pyramidschemebar.com
• • • •
HOPCAT
Grand Rapids, Michigan
hopcatgr.com
• • • •
ASHLEY'S
Ann Arbor and
Westland, Michigan
ashleys.com
• • • •
ONE EYED BETTY'S
Ferndale, Michigan
oneeyedbettys.com
• • • •
PEARL'S
Elk Rapids, Michigan
magnumhospitality.com/pearls
• • • •
CITY PARK GRILL
Petoskey, Michigan
cityparkgrill.com
• • • •
TRATTORIA STELLA
Traverse City, Michigan
stellatc.com
• • • •
7 MONKS
Traverse City, Michigan
7monkstap.com

Michigan Beer

Today it's hard to imagine people *not* coming in droves for a limited, highly crafted set of 13 one-off beers from Short's. In the years since the Imperial Beer Series, Short's has gained a near-cult status with many of its followers. But when the brewery first arrived, it was doing something relatively unfamiliar in the area.

A big part of arriving at a small town in northern Michigan and introducing extraordinarily flavorful beer was educating beer drinkers about what they were doing. "In order to get people to appreciate what we did, we had to be creative, educate them, and invest in them," Joe says. "The more energy and time spent on customers, the more they will come back, the more they will share their story."

Joe started with five beers on tap. "Being in this demographic, I knew we had to have a light lager, and because we didn't have wine, we needed something fruity, and if I was going to be drinking beer here, we needed an IPA," Joe said. So he covered all the bases to get his foundation.

Even though his brewery needed that foundation, creativity was always the essential part of what drove Joe to open it. "The interest for me in being able to control what we produced in the brewery was solely the love of experimentation," he says. Though he thrives on never doing the same thing twice, Joe understood the necessity of consistency. Brewmaster Tony Hansen has been essential in achieving that consistency.

Joe met Tony through the brewpub's homebrew club. Tony had come to a few meetings and expressed an interest in working with Joe.

"His interview was two questions: 'Can you cook, and can you fix your own car?'" says Joe, who considered the job as brewer as part mechanical and part culinary. Tony answered: "I've been a line cook for eight years, and I just converted my car to vegetable oil."

Tony and Joe found their balance: Tony standardized recipes and organized the process, and Joe continued to pursue his extreme creativity. In early spring 2012 the brewery hit its 1,000th batch of Huma Lupa Licious. To celebrate, it made an extremely limited, bottle-conditioned double version of Huma (ABV 12.8 percent) and called it Aww Jeah. It took Short's three years to brew and sell its first 1,000 batches of Huma

Lupa Licious but less than a year for its second 1,000. As a tradition, Joe is considering doubling a different beer for each major anniversary mark.

There isn't much Joe and Tony won't consider when it comes to brewing beer: the 2013 beer production schedule listed 28 limited-release beers, in addition to their four seasonals and five flagships.

Despite having a wide-reaching range of beer styles, Short's reins it in geographically: its beer is only available in Michigan. "Keeping it close to home means we have a handle on quality: we know who sells it, who buys it, and we can make 50 beers a year if we want—that's the fun part, the part we got into this for," Joe says. "It's never been about being a dominating brewery. It's about doing what we love, where we want to live. The fact that we are operating a world-class brewing operation in north-western lower Michigan in a town of 1,400 people—that's the biggest feather in my hat."

The Irreplaceable

Within eight years of starting Short's, Joe got married, bought a house, got a puppy, renovated the house, and had two kids—all the while expanding the brewery and building a crew of supportive and hardworking employees. Joe is as persistent as Jim May when he knows what he wants.

> **BREWER'S PLAYLIST**
>
> **JOHN HARTFORD** • Back in the Goodle Days
> **JOHN HARTFORD** • Get No Better
> **MY MORNING JACKET** • Touch Me I'm Going to Scream, Pt. 2
> **WILCO** • Handshake Drugs
> **WEEN** • Band On the Run (Wings cover)
> **WEEN** • The Argus (Live in Chicago)
> **FLEET FOXES** • White Winter Hymnal
> **ANDREW BIRD** • Masterfade
> **BECK** • Lost Cause
> **BREATHE OWL BREATHE** • Sabre Tooth Tiger
> **GREG BROWN** • Who Woulda Thunk It?
> **BUILT TO SPILL** • Liar
> **DR. DOG** • Jackie Wants a Black Eye
> **FRUIT BATS** • Seaweed
> **YUKON BLONDE** • Blood Cops
> **ILLINOIS** • Nosebleed
> **BAND OF HORSES** • The Funeral
> **WILCO** • Either Way
> **CAKE** • The Guitar Man (Bread cover)
> **THAO & THE GET DOWN STAY DOWN** • Bag of Hammers

Joe's wife, Leah, has been there for most of the journey. "Joe acts on his daydreams immediately and you're doing it the next day," Leah says. "If he doesn't see progress in 24 to 48 hours, he starts doing it himself." Like hand-bottling, hang-tagging, and hand-signing thousands of bottles of beer. Creative drive isn't the extra for Joe, Leah says, it's the necessary.

Leah says it's like Joe is floating way up above the clouds in a land of creativity, and she is holding onto his feet. If hers can be just barely dragging along the ground, then they are reaching their balance. "If it weren't for him, these ideas and projects would never happen," she says. "And if it weren't for me, they'd happen in excess and we'd have gone under.

"I do my job very well, but Joe defines the image, the brand—everything. He is the irreplaceable."

SURLY BREWING COMPANY

BROOKLYN CENTER AND MINNEAPOLIS, MINNESOTA

Surly isn't just making beer, it's making laws. Thanks to the "Surly Bill," in May 2011 every brewery in Minnestoa was permitted to start serving pints on site.

Before the law passed, Minnesota breweries producing more than 3,500 barrels a year weren't allowed to sell beer at their own facilities due to the restrictive three-tier system that separates manufacturers, distributors, and retailers. Surly mobilized local supporters to help fight against the Minnesota Licensed Beverage Association (MLBA) and to allow breweries to serve without restrictions. The MLBA eventually relented when lawmakers agreed to limit the bill so that only breweries making fewer than 250,000 barrels a year were permitted to apply for a license to serve on their premises.

Surly's efforts helped breweries across the state, but owner and instigator Omar Ansari can't take credit for being entirely altruistic: much of the motivation to change the law in the first place was born of Surly's plans for a new $20 million destination brewery of its own in Minneapolis. Plans include a production facility, restaurant, beer garden, and rooftop terrace—whose existence depended on the ability to drink beer on site, legally.

Owner
OMAR ANSARI

Brewmaster
TODD HAUG

Established
2005

Production Volume
20,000 BARRELS (2012)

Distribution
MINNESOTA

Website
surlybrewing.com

Beer with an Attitude

If there were a brewery that could overturn a law, Surly would be it.

Years ago, Omar and his wife were traveling around in Portland, Oregon, on a beer trip, enjoying the good local beer that was everywhere. When they returned to Minneapolis they were frustrated with the limited availability of good beer. "We say you get mad—or surly—from the inability to find good beer," says brewmaster Todd Haug. Omar decided to make his own good beer.

Todd was working at Rock Bottom Brewery when he heard from a common friend that Omar was starting a brewery and needed someone to put the brewhouse together. Omar brought Todd on board at the end of 2005, and Surly started selling beer the next year.

When Todd and Omar partnered up to open the brewery, Todd had been in the industry since he was 21 and Omar was a homebrewer with a manufacturing background. "It was the perfect opportunity for Omar because he was naïve about the industry, which was great because it didn't deter him," Todd says. "He just said, 'I don't care what anybody says, I'm going to do it.'"

From the beginning, the goal was for drinkers to have a fresh start with Surly. Omar and Todd wanted to make people remember the beer—whether they liked it or not—just as long as the beer was well made. To ensure that fresh start, Omar and Todd intentionally didn't do what other American craft breweries were doing.

"With Furious and Bender, we wanted names that didn't hearken to the US craft beer scene: no animals, no wildlife," Todd says. "We also didn't want to pigeonhole our beers with style designations." When you pick up a can of Furious, an American IPA, you won't see the IPA designation.

Todd says he knows drinkers who say that they don't like IPAs, but that they love Furious. "Somewhere along the line they had an IPA that they didn't like," he says. "We wanted to get away from that badge. We wanted people to decide on their own based on the way the beer tasted, not what they think it's supposed to be."

Get a Pint

THE HAPPY GNOME
St. Paul, Minnesota
thehappygnome.com

• • • •

BUTCHER AND THE BOAR
Minneapolis, Minnesota
butcherandtheboar.com

• • • •

MACKENZIE PUB
Minneapolis, Minnesota
mackenziepub.com

• • • •

MUDDY WATERS
Minneapolis, Minnesota
muddywatersmpls.com

• • • •

ZEN BOX IZAKAYA
Minneapolis, Minnesota
zenboxizakaya.com

That has both worked and not worked. A drinker once spit a mouthful of Furious out at Omar, accusing him of not telling him it was an IPA. But for the most part, it has worked with Furious. With the brewery's Bitter Brewer, it backfired. Bitter Brewer refers to the style of beer, and not a flavor descriptor, which has confused people and turned many away from what they fear is beer with an overwhelmingly bitter taste. But there are those who know what it is and what it is supposed to be, Todd says, and they love it.

Furious

It didn't take long for Surly to find a crew of loyal—and at times fanatic—followers. With that have come a lot of opinions. Surly's fans want Furious, and are just short of furious themselves that the brewery won't increase production on the favorite brew.

Todd says it's been challenging to hold production of Furious back so that they can make all of the beer styles he and his brewers want to brew.

"We don't sit around and drink Furious all day," he laughs. "We drink small beers and session beers. I'd rather have three or five beers than a couple of huge ones. I like the variety. I like to have a malt-forward beer and then switch to an IPA."

But the Furious fever still spreads like wildfire among Surly's surly fans. After the brewery announced it would be making Hell year round, bloggers and commentators were quick to get online and complain the brewery wasn't upping production on one of the bigger beers. But Todd stands his ground and says he and his brewers love Hell, which is a challenging and rewarding beer to make.

"We take a lot of pride in making a clean, well-made lager," says Todd, who wants to be able to reach drinkers beyond their biggest fans. "In order to get into the next tier of beer drinkers, I don't care if they ever drink Furious, but if they like Hell and they know it's from Minnesota, then we've connected with a local consumer," he says.

The Minnesota beer drinker has become Surly's entire focus. The brewery pulled out of Chicago and other markets in 2010, trying to keep up with its buyers in Minnesota and to meet local demand, which Todd says is hard to manage.

"They say, 'Why don't you make more?' But there isn't a spigot that just makes more beer," Todd says. "It takes labor, training, raw materials." Surly's raw materials aren't available all the time—like specialty and increasingly hard-to-get hops—and if expanded production requires the use of whatever ingredients are available, the consistency of its beers will change.

When Surly does relocate to its new production facility, Surly drinkers will likely get some of the bigger batches of Furious that they have been wanting: Surly's 30-barrel brewhouse will become a 100-barrel brewhouse; 60-barrel fermenters will be replaced by 600-barrel fermenters. The new facility will increase capacity to 100,000 barrels, putting the brewery closer to the size of larger Minnesota breweries like August Schell's and the Summit Brewing Company.

Darkness and Specialty Brews

Of the 20,000 barrels Surly had planned to make in 2013, only 240 barrels were slated to be its Russian imperial stout Darkness. It's a tiny amount of beer that takes a ton of work to make—in part because the labor-intensive and inefficient brewing process takes over all of the brewery's equipment, and in part because Surly changes the bottle

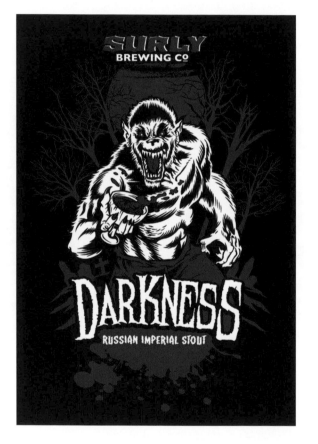

design every year. Darkness is released one day a year, on Darkness Day, and it's sold out in hours.

Darkness Day is to Surly what Dark Lord Day is to Indiana's Three Floyds: a single and much-anticipated day filled with excited and eager drinkers hoping for a place far up enough in line to get a bottle of the rare release.

Every year Surly also makes an anniversary beer that gets bottled in large-format bottles. For its fifth anniversary in 2012, Surly released Pentagram, which is 100 percent *Brettanomyces*-fermented beer. *Brettanomyces*, or "Brett," is a wild yeast frequently used in certain Belgian ales, with flavor profiles often described as *barnyard* or *funky*.

There weren't many—if any—brewers in Minnesota who had used Brett on the scale Surly had, and Todd says they received a lot of emails from people saying something was wrong with the beer because of that sour, funky, barnyard flavor. "This beer is not timid," Todd says. "So if you don't know what that is, and you went and spent a bunch of money on the beer, you think something is wrong. We wanted to say with the label: don't buy this just because it's Surly."

Indeed, the label has a "Beware!" warning: "This Arcane Seal guards an enigmatic brew that is FUNKY, DARK, and SOUR. If you choose to break the seal, YOU HAVE BEEN WARNED!"

Although most of Surly's beers show up on the market in cans, the specialty beers suitable for aging are packaged in bottle format. They are all more than 8 percent ABV, with waxed tops and silkscreened designs. "It's a good way to educate people," Todd says. "Bottles, thanks to wine, have that more elevated sense of aging and special occasions; the beer in cans is beer that is ready to drink, so drink it as fresh as possible."

Surly has been packaging in cans
since the beginning.

Cans

When Surly started in 2005, few craft breweries were packing beer in cans, but they have always appealed to Todd. "I remember looking at trade mags and telling Omar, 'Someday you're going to have your beer in cans.' He laughed and was like, 'No way—cans are for crappy beer.'"

Todd insisted. The equipment had gotten better and was more available. His wife had the idea to do 16-ounce cans, like a pub pour. When Surly started packaging beyond kegs, its beer was in cans.

Todd says the cost is essentially equal between bottling and canning. With bottles, one-offs are an easy option: all you need to do is print the labels. With cans, you have to commit to a certain number since they need to be manufactured in large pallets. Because of that limiting factor, it took Surly awhile to get the production value up to the point of being able to add more brands.

Every weekend 300 to 400 people tour through Surly. Todd says someone always asks when they are going to switch from cans to bottles, as if it's a baby step and not an intentional decision.

"We've just always liked cans," he says. "It's part of our whole attitude: we're doing it because we like it, not because it's cool, but because we like it.

"Some of the best music is created by people who create it because it's an extension of them, not because they want to sell records," Todd continues. "We're trying hard to stay focused on that, because we believe we have a lot of cool ideas, and a lot of people seem to agree with us. It's worked out pretty well."

BREWER'S PLAYLIST

GOATWHORE
• Beyond the Spell of Discontent

GRAVEYARD
• Satan's Finest

1349
• Atomic Chapel

BLOODBATH
• Eaten

ARCHGOAT
• Blessed Vulva

CARCASS
• Lavaging Expectorate of Lysergide Composition

WITCHCRAFT
• The Alchemist

SERPENTINE PATH
• Compendium of Suffering

YOB
• Burning the Altar

VADER
• Devilizer

HIGH ON FIRE
• Frost Hammer

SKELETONWITCH
• Cleaver of Souls

SATYRICON
• K.I.N.G.

HOODED MENACE
• Effigies of Evil

SAHG
• Godless Faith

METROPOLITAN BREWING

CHICAGO, ILLINOIS

Doug Hurst received an A for the first beer he ever made. He was taking a botany class called Plants and Man at the University of Wisconsin–Madison, and students were given the choice to write a term paper or do a project. Doug had heard brewing was an option: Why write a term paper when you could brew beer?

He and a classmate went to the local brew shop, bought a kit, and made beer for the class. "We did get an A," he laughs. But the appeal stayed with him even as the class ended. "I was really interested and intrigued by the process," Doug says. "There was something about making my own that I really enjoyed, and something in those early batches that I could taste, and I wanted to figure that out."

The Beginning

In 2001 Doug was at a beer festival in Chicago with a friend he had homebrewed with years before, a friend who had once suggested they open a brewery. Doug brought it up once again, and said they should open a brewery. His friend laughed it off, but Doug didn't let go of the idea.

In 2003 Doug attended the Siebel Institute of Technology in Chicago. He had been homebrewing for a decade but wanted to complement his knowledge with the technical and industrial side of brewing. "As a homebrewer you learn about ingredients and

Founders
DOUG HURST, TRACY HURST

Brewmaster
DOUG HURST

Established
2007

Production Volume
3,000 BARRELS (2012)

Distribution
ILLINOIS

Website
metrobrewing.com

the different styles of beer," he says, "but you don't learn how to produce consistently in a quality manner. That's what Siebel teaches."

Doug considered brewing jobs after school but came to realize quickly that he wanted to run his own brewery. He began to write a business plan for Metropolitan. Soon he and Tracy Hurst—his current business partner and then wife—began to put together the brewery; built out a warehouse space in the Ravenswood neighborhood of Chicago; and, in January 2009, shipped their first beer.

Lagers

It was important to Doug to have a focus and to make a statement with the beer he brewed. From the beginning, Metropolitan's statement has been that lagers are flavorful.

"When I was in Germany studying brewing, I was drinking German lagers like Hacker-Pschorr, and they tasted a whole lot better," Doug says. "The reason is freshness; their beer gets here and it's not the same anymore." Doug gained an appreciation for how much subtlety and variety there is in lighter-colored beers, and he became intrigued with creating that freshness and quality back home.

Doug thought about the Midwest and cities like Chicago, Milwaukee, and St. Louis—cities where German immigrants came in the mid-19th century and started breweries and made their beer from home: lagers. Several of those became famous, big-name places: Schlitz, Pabst, Anheuser-Busch.

"I looked around and saw these industrial beers that destroyed the name of lager, because there is so much to a lager," Doug says. "And then I saw the craft brewers who have taken British beer styles and turned them into something completely, uniquely American."

Doug noticed that when craft brewers made lagers, they tended to brew them as close to the style as possible. Yet the same craft brewer might make an IPA and use

Get a Pint

SMALL BAR
Chicago, Illinois
thesmallbar.com
• • • •
THE MAP ROOM
Chicago, Illinois
maproom.com
• • • •
HOPLEAF
Chicago, Illinois
hopleaf.com
• • • •
CLARK STREET ALE HOUSE
Chicago, Illinois
clarkstreetalehouse.com

way more hops than the British did. He wanted to take that same inventive approach, but with lagers.

Metropolitan came out with Dynamo Copper Lager and Flywheel Bright Lager. Both were inspired by specific beer styles, yet neither was strictly to style. Flywheel resembles a Dortmunder or a German pilsner—a lager modeled after a pale ale; Dynamo was modeled after a Vienna-style lager—an amber beer with a toasty character and malty richness.

Much of the inspiration for Metropolitan beers comes from German or European styles. Krankshaft Kölsch is in the style of beer from Cologne, Germany, where more than 20 breweries all make a version of the same beer. Kölsch uses an ale yeast but ferments colder, goes through a cold conditioning period like a lager, and ferments

for about the same amount of time as a lager. The result, Doug says, is a beer that is clean like a lager, but with a fruity, flowery aroma. Krankshaft is one of Metropolitan's bestsellers. "I didn't set out to make a mass-appeal beer, but it seems to have taken off that way," Doug says.

Metropolitan's Ironworks Alt is modeled after the beer made in Düsseldorf, Germany, about 30 miles north of Cologne. Also a hybrid ale-lager brewed with the same yeast as kölsch, it's a darker beer with a hoppier profile. The two towns are extremely competitive about their two styles: there is no alt served in Cologne, no kölsch served in Düsseldorf.

Doug at his 15-barrel brewhouse, pre-expansion.

"You have multiple breweries making the same kind of beer, with this funny rivalry," Doug says. "I thought, we don't do rivalries here—we're all good friends with other brewers in other places, so we're going to make both styles of beer, in the same brewery."

Chicago

In the years when Metropolitan was preparing to open, craft beer in Chicago was relatively small. Tracy and Doug spent time visiting other breweries across the country, learning about the industry, and touring equipment manufacturers. At that time in Chicago, there were no production-only breweries. Brewpubs like Piece and Rock Bottom Brewery and Goose Island were doing well, but Tracy and Doug wanted to be a production-only company.

Trekkie tanks: many breweries name fermenters instead of giving them numbers.

There was never a question to open anywhere but the city. "I think cities are one of humanity's greatest inventions. They bring people together. They accomplish great things: gigantic buildings or industry or high technology or great universities. Cities are magical," Doug says. "We are celebrating the idea of a city."

BREWER'S PLAYLIST

MASTODON • Curl of the Burl

BEASTIE BOYS • Egg Man

RED FANG • Prehistoric Dog

MOTÖRHEAD • Ace of Spades

HIGH ON FIRE • The Face of Oblivion

FUGAZI • Waiting Room

RUSH • Working Man

MINUTEMEN • This Ain't No Picnic

FATBOY SLIM • Weapon of Choice

MODEST MOUSE • Tiny Cities Made of Ashes

RAGE AGAINST THE MACHINE • Pistol Grip Pump

THE MELVINS • Revolve

SLEEP • Holy Mountain

SLAYER • Disciple

BLACK SABBATH • Hand of Doom

PANTERA • Yesterday Don't Mean Shit

NAILBOMB • World of Shit

REFUSED • Refused Are Fucking Dead

POLVO • Beggar's Bowl

HÜSKER DÜ • I'll Never Forget You

At the time, Tracy says, it was "uncool" to open a brewery in Chicago, and it was uncool to do lagers. Someone on Beer Advocate's site even wrote that Metropolitan wasn't the trendiest brewery. "We're not," Tracy says. "We like to say, 'Beer for the Proletariat.' We're the beer you drink at the bar after work with your friends."

Doug and Tracy take pride in making lagers that are both sessionable and interesting and in redeeming lagers. "Just because the macros ruined the reputation of lagers doesn't take away from what it is," she says. "When we put out a bock and people say, 'Is this a lager?', we can say, as a matter of fact it is, and how awesome is it?"

Freshness is one of the most important pieces to what Metropolitan does, and it's the key factor that determines distribution. Doug says they plan to extend distribution from solely northeastern Illinois to include a few neighboring states, with the ultimate goal of being a regional brewery, not shipping beer much farther than a day's drive. Doug and Tracy cite New Glarus as a role model—"the holy grail" of making local, fresh beer: it doesn't ship outside of Wisconsin, and yet it's producing more than 125,000 barrels a year.

Metropolitan produced just under 3,000 barrels in 2012, and by 2013 it was underway with an expansion that would allow it to increase production to as many as 7,000 barrels. Doug says the increase in production won't affect the plan to keep the beer close to home. "If we felt the need to go outside of the Midwest," Doug says, "We'd build a new brewery, rather than ship across the country."

A Call to Make Good Beer

Despite what anyone has said online, in the time since the brewery opened, it's become "cool" that Metropolitan does one thing, and one thing well. In a market increasingly flooded with breweries that tend to do a lot at once, Doug and Tracy are admired for narrowing their attention and focusing their efforts.

They say they welcome the surge in craft beer, something Doug attributes largely to the Millennial generation coming of age: a generation for whom craft beer has always been around rather than something new to discover. "It just is," he says. "And as soon as they can afford it, they buy more and more of it."

They also welcome the new breweries coming to Chicago—more than 76 were on the drawing board at the beginning of 2013—with one caveat: the beer has to be good.

"We worked really hard to establish this reputation, and if people are going to make beer that doesn't taste good, it's going to reverse a lot of that," Tracy says. "The onus to make reliable beer is massive; but as long as people are cranking out good liquid, I'm in."

5 RABBIT CERVECERIA, INC.

BEDFORD PARK, ILLINOIS

The idea for 5 Rabbit came from a relatively simple thought: If Latin America is so culturally rich, why were its beers so tasteless and bland? Costa Rican–born Andres Araya and Mexican-born Isaac Showaki were determined to make beers packed not just with flavor but also with the flavorful culture and history of Latin America.

Andres and Isaac met in Mexico City in 2006 while working at an international consulting firm, assigned to the same account: one of Latin America's largest breweries. One night, Andres, Isaac, and the brewery's brand managers were working late. They ordered some beer—three of their own brand and three of their competitor's—and had a blind taste test.

"That was a disaster," Andres says. "One of the brand managers liked his brand the least, and his competitor's the best." Andres later told his wife, Mila, about the tasting. "Not only are these beers bland and boring," he said, "but you can't even tell them apart—not even the people who are supposed to know."

Andres points to Latin America's rich food, history, and colorful web of cultural influences. "You can say a lot of things about Latin America, but you cannot say it's boring," Andres says. "When you think of Latin American beers and you think those are boring, there is a disconnect." He started working on a plan for a new, Latin American–influenced brewery.

Owners
ANDRES ARAYA,
RANDY MOSHER

Brewmaster
JOHN J. HALL

Established
2011

Production Volume
3,000 BARRELS (2012)

Distribution
ILLINOIS
OHIO
PENNSYLVANIA

Website
5rabbitbrewery.com

Andres Araya and brewmaster John J. Hall just days before bottling the first beer at the new Bedford Park brewery.

5 Rabbit

Andres was in Florida and Isaac in New York when they decided to move to Chicago to start their brewery. Andres had gone to Purdue University and was familiar with the city. It was home to a burgeoning craft beer scene and a strong Latino community, and it seemed like the right spot for 5 Rabbit.

In Aztec mythology, 5 Rabbit is one of the leaders of the 400 Rabbits, the children of Mayahuel (the goddess of maguey, or agave) and Patecatl (the god of fermentation). Along with 5 Grass, 5 Flower, 5 Lizard, and 5 Vulture, 5 Rabbit is one of the five deities who symbolize excess (Ahuiateteo). The pleasure gods are reminders to enjoy life's indulgences, but in moderation.

5 Rabbit started with Mexican mythology, but Andres says it is influenced by Latin America as a whole, from the southern tip of Chile to northern Mexico, and even the Caribbean. "We started with pre-Hispanic Mexico, but we want to move into other eras," he says. They have made beers influenced by northern Colombia, Venezuela, and Central America—influenced geographically as well as by moments in time.

Brewing beer from a cultural angle is a different approach than most take; the approach 5 Rabbit is taking is almost entirely removed from the style of beer itself. Early on, Andres and Isaac found just the right partner to help guide them in their less-than-conventional direction.

Andres and Isaac came to Chicago in 2010 for a beer author's event at the Map Room, where they met Ray Daniels, founder of the Cicerone Certification Program; Jeff Sparrow, brewer and author; and other members of Chicago's burgeoning craft beer community. "Mila spent most of the night talking to this other guy, and after we left she said we had to talk to him," Andres remembers. They called him that night to meet the next day for lunch. That other guy was Randy Mosher.

Randy is a well-known Chicago beer writer and the author of *Radical Brewing*, *Brewer's Companion,* and *Tasting Beer*, as well as a brewer himself and a graphic designer. He had everything Andres and Isaac could use, and the three hit it off. By October 2010, Randy was a full-fledged part of the brewery, and he began to work on design and labels as well as the beer recipes.

The following year, Goose Island brewer John J. Hall was at an event during Chicago Craft Beer Week at Garfield Park Conservatory, where he first came into contact with 5 Rabbit. The upstart brewery had just rolled out its beer. "I'd never heard of it, and I saw the two of them and Randy Mosher," John says. "I thought, 'What's Randy doing over there with these people and who are these people and what the heck is 5 Vulture?'"

John, who was once Randy's student at the Siebel Institute of Technology in Chicago, says he was excited that Randy was a part of the new brewery. A few months later, John left his 15-year career at Goose Island and signed on as brewmaster at 5 Rabbit.

Get a Pint

THE GREEN LADY
Chicago, Illinois
thegreenlady-chicago.com
• • • •
SIMONE'S BAR
Chicago, Illinois
simonesbar.com
• • • •
STATE AND LAKE
Chicago, Illinois
stateandlakechicago.com
• • • •
VILLAGE TAP
Chicago, Illinois
thevillagetap.com

John is on board with the brewery's radical approach to beer, and brewing with specialty ingredients like hibiscus, piloncillo sugar, and Tasmanian pepper berries. Searching South America for rare ingredients, Randy recently traveled up the Amazon, seeking out river fruits and other indigenous flavors to use in 5 Rabbit's brews. Because 5 Rabbit is small, it doesn't need large quantities to do experimental batches, which means it doesn't run into problems sourcing large quantities of rare materials.

Bottling Its Own

It's the last week of 2012, and the brewery is getting ready to bottle its first batch of beer. Beer is in the fermenters at the new production facility, and the brewers have

teased the bright tank with water and done a test run with their bottling line. They're anxious to start making the beer themselves.

Although 5 Rabbit was released to the market in 2011, it started out contract-brewing, a decision influenced by a conservative business plan. The original plan was to build its own production facility within three years, but after 5 Rabbit's beer was so well-received across the city during the first year—it even picked up a deal with Chipotle to sell beer in Chicago locations—it bumped up its schedule, found a building on the south side, and started buying equipment.

Though its current goal is 6,000 barrels a year, John says the capacity could take 5 Rabbit to as many as 44,000 barrels. For now, the focus is on building the brand,

5 Rabbit brews with unusual ingredients, like chamomile flowers; the brewery's packaging and finishing line.

making beer, and continuing to pursue the company's creative approach to brewing—an innovative spirit that extends through all parts of what the team is doing. For example, Isaac and Andres were stumped when they tried to find tap handles within budget. Randy went to his workshop for a solution and began to make the handles himself. Today handcrafted 5 Rabbit tap handles can be found around the city, no one exactly like the other: craft tap handles for craft beer.

The Future

Although it seemed like smooth sailing from the start—snagging both Randy and John and moving up the three-year plan because business was so good—the brewery hit bumps in late 2012 when a litigious fight between cofounders Isaac and Andres resulted in their split. After months of legal battles, Isaac sold his majority stake.

Soon after, Cesar Garza came on as commercial director in charge of sales and marketing.

It's likely 5 Rabbit's drinkers won't bat an eye at the temporary turmoil that overtook the brewery, as long as the beer itself maintains its quality and reputation for being something new in the craft beer marketplace.

During his years at Goose Island, John watched the Midwest craft beer evolution, which started with a big focus on hops, then moved on to barrel aging and then to sour beers, Belgian–style beers, and lambics. Now the question is, what's next? "I'm not saying we are niche-ing, but we are trying to find a new direction," he says. "The common thread of what we do is doing a lot of different things."

John says he thinks the current trend is collaboration, marrying two different breweries with two different styles of beer to make something entirely new. In fact, Randy had just made plans for 5 Rabbit to brew together with Indiana's Three Floyds.

"We can't do what Floyd does, and he can't do what we do," John says. "Floyd tends to go over the top; we're doing interesting Latin flavors—so what are we going to do together? I have no idea; we'll have to drink a few beers and decide that."

BREWER'S PLAYLIST

THE JAZZ BUTCHER
- Soul Happy Hour
- Drink
- Partytime
- Down the Drain
- Water

SQUEEZE
- I Won't Ever Go Drinking Again (best hangover song, ever)

JON FRATELLI
- Daddy Won't Pay Your Bill Tonight

XTC
- We're All Light

NEIL AND TIM FINN
- Paradise (Wherever You Are)

SWEET
- Ballroom Blitz

THE KINGS
- Switchin' to Glide

T-REX
- 20th Century Boy

THE WONDER STUFF
- Ten Trenches Deep (live)

FOCUS
- Hocus Pocus

OK GO
- All Is Not Lost

OINGO BOINGO
- Grey Matter

THE FRATELLIS
- Everybody Knows You Cried Last Night

SHRIEKBACK
- Feelers (live)

THE SPECIALS
- Enjoy Yourself

KING BISCUIT TIME
- I Walk the Earth

GREENBUSH BREWING COMPANY

SAWYER, MICHIGAN

hen Justin Heckathorn and Scott Sullivan started Greenbush, they figured they'd open a small brewery and taproom in Sawyer, Michigan—a town of just more than 2,000—doing what they loved, making beer, hopefully making a few bucks to support a living. They were nowhere near prepared for what happened instead.

Scott was a woodworker living in Chicago, doing contract furniture and lighting when he nearly cut off his finger late in 2007. Waiting for his hand to heal, he found himself with twelve weeks to kill. "I don't sit still very well, so I started homebrewing," he says.

People kept telling Scott his beer was so good he could sell it, and soon enough he was brewing full time. In early 2009 he met Jill Sites, who owned a wine shop in Chicago. Jill put on a regular beer fest and invited Scott to participate. She fell in love with his beer and started working with Justin and Scott on the beginnings of what would be Greenbush Brewing Company. Soon Scott was doing regular events and beer tastings throughout Chicago and southwestern Michigan, making as much beer and trying to create as much buzz as he could. Scott took his beer to Extreme Beer Fest in Three Oaks, Michigan, and was cleaned out immediately. Justin and Scott started to write a business plan to open a brewery in Sawyer and started to look for space and investors.

Owners
JUSTIN HECKATHORN,
JILL SITES,
SCOTT SULLIVAN

Brewmasters
SCOTT SULLIVAN,
JOSEPH HINMAN

Established
2011

Production Volume
11,000 BARRELS (2013)

Distribution
ILLINOIS
INDIANA
MICHIGAN

Website
greenbushbrewing.com

Scott Sullivan (left), Jill Sites, and Justin Heckathorn (right) outside their Sawyer, Michigan, brewery and taproom.

At the end of 2009, they took over a building in Sawyer and gutted it. During construction, Scott was endlessly brewing—out of his kitchen or garage or any space he could find. He was approaching chefs and restaurants throughout Chicago, handing out beer.

When Justin, Scott, and Jill finally opened the 32-person taproom in 2011, the idea was it was going to be a tasting room. Scott would brew in the back and come to the taproom to serve people who came in for tastings. "We thought I'd sell beer to go when people came in—we thought it would be a dusty little shop that we'd grow slowly."

But during the couple of years leading up to the opening, Scott had handed out 9,000 bottles of beer. He had created a lot of buzz. Three hundred and fifty people showed up for the soft opening for family and friends. More than 500 people came through the taproom the next day, Greenbush's official opening.

Three weeks later, during the Fourth of July weekend, Greenbush ran out of beer. Justin, Scott, and Jill realized they had to make beer, and a lot of it, and their subpar fermenters weren't going to work. They threw out their original plan, hired a new brewer and bartenders, and bought new fermenters.

Their one-year plan was to do 375 barrels. Instead, they brewed 2,347 barrels: nearly seven times their projection. The next year, in 2012, production was up to 4,200 barrels. They had only been open for 18 months when they were projecting their 2013 production volume at 11,000 barrels. So much for dusty little shop.

When Greenbush first started serving beer out of its taproom, it had a meat and cheese plate and pretzels to accompany it. By the end of 2012 they had invested in a convection oven, a pizza station, and a full-time chef. Food has become 30 percent

of business, and Greenbush sources from local farms like Granor and Iron Creek whenever it can. One day Scott brought his smoker over to the brewery and smoked four briskets. In four hours, on a Saturday in January, 50 pounds of meat disappeared. Greenbush subsequently bought a smoker and started smoking meat out back.

It was clear early on that the small taproom Greenbush originally opened wouldn't accommodate the constant flow of people. Halfway through the first year, it finished a taproom expansion. On snowy Saturdays in February, Jill says they started to see nearly 100 people packing the room.

Somewhere along the line, Scott and Justin made Jill—who had been doing everything from marketing to cleaning kegs—a full-time partner.

The Beer

"While Scott was brewing the 9,000 bottles of beer he handed out, he was constantly working on his recipes," Jill says. "In truth we still work on our recipes. There are people who come in and say Red Bud tastes different—but it's better. We're a small craft brewer, and I want our beers to taste better every time you drink them." By the time Greenbush opened, Scott was brewing 35 different beers, making them over and over again to perfect the recipes. Jill likes to say what Greenbush does is a restrained, classical experimentation.

Scott agrees. "That's true, because my view is that you should never be afraid to try anything, but you should think about what you are doing.

"There are always purists, and that kind of methodology tells you to pay attention to your variables and process—that's good," Scott says. "But German brewing technique

would never let you put spice or fruit in a beer, and that is BS. The measure of a good beer is not whether it meets a style guide but is, do you like it, does it taste good?"

Scott doesn't ever brew within style guidelines. When he created Anger, a black IPA and one of the flagships, instead of using debittered black malt, Scott used regular black malt and chocolate malt, because he had a lot around from brewing porters and stouts. He decided to modify, and it has turned out to be one of Greenbush's most successful beers.

The building used to be a laundromat, panini shop, and video store before Greenbush took it over in 2009.

He's also brewed a beer that tastes just like an old-fashioned cocktail, first using an aromatics recipe that goes into the boil, and then aging it in Templeton Rye barrels. "I would serve that with a cherry and an orange," Scott jokes.

Delusion, Greenbush's flagship barrel beer, is released in 22-ounce bombers once a year in the week before Christmas. Two hundred bottles sold out in a handful of hours in 2012. Production was upped to 1,200 bombers for 2013.

"We are willing to try anything but like to make sure it has some classical tradition to it," Scott says. "We don't want to throw a bunch of—" He stops himself mid-sentence and then laughs. "I was about to say, 'You don't want to throw a bunch of mushrooms in a beer,' but I guess we just did that and it was really good."

Scott's flavors are bold and big, but smooth and balanced. A self-taught brewer, Scott has been cooking since he was barely three years old, and his love of culinary

Club members' mugs hang from the ceiling of the taproom; tap handles at the bar; beer aging in Templeton Rye barrels.

flavors and wide-ranging ingredients inspires his recipes. A father of four, and a relentlessly hard worker, Scott comes across as a sweet guy—a passionate brewer with a humble demeanor. Yet his arsenal of beer comes with aggressive, dark names—including Anger, Distortion, and Retribution—with equally bellicose bottle art.

"In the midst of this, I managed to lose my house, leave Chicago, go bankrupt—it was a really bad couple of years," Scott says. "I was working really hard to build something out of it. I wasn't going to just sit down and die, but I was really, really crabby about what was going on."

He did build something out of it. Greenbush is more than just a wildly successful new brewery: it's also a gathering place for the community and surrounding area.

A Community

"The whole point is that we love what we do, but we love the idea of bettering this area and working with local farms and local chefs," Jill says. "We are the very accidental anchor to a lot of everything around here." It's true: Greenbush has created a public house environment. Justin and Scott both have families of four young kids, and Greenbush's space is for beer geeks and tourists, locals and their families, and people of all ages.

The brewery has strived to think about the whole package: the beer, the food, and its staff of 40—most of whom are locals who went to high school together. "We have given them a reason to stay," Jill says, "and that's how you turn around an economy. We want this to be successful for everybody, and not just for Greenbush."

STEEL TOE BREWING

ST. LOUIS PARK, MINNESOTA

reweries in the Midwest are exploding with growth right now. Nearly every brewery is in the middle of construction, adding fermenters, increasing the size of the brewhouse, buying new bottling lines, putting up new buildings, or moving all together.

But not Jason Schoneman, owner and brewmaster of Steel Toe Brewery. Quality, consistency, and a focus on his local community are Jason's goals for Steel Toe. And he has no intention to grow beyond 3,500 barrels a year.

10 Years

Jason spent 10 careful and deliberate years to get where he is today. He grew up inspired by his mom, who ran her own business, and since he was little he has wanted to run his own—although he didn't know then that beer would be his business.

His first awareness of beer was when he spent a few years in Colorado hanging out, enjoying the outdoors, and tasting great beer. By the mid-'90s he had moved back to his home state of Iowa and couldn't find anything like what he had been drinking. So he started brewing his own.

In 2000 Jason followed his girlfriend, now wife, back west and ended up in Montana, where he started working for Lightning Boy Brewery. He began with packaging. Next he moved to the bottling line. Two weeks later he was brewing.

Owner
SCHONEMAN FAMILY

Head Brewer
JASON SCHONEMAN

Established
2011

Production Volume
>1,000 BARRELS (2012)

Distribution
MINNESOTA

Website
steeltoebrewing.com

He stayed there for a year, working long, exhausting days brewing and bottling and loading as fast as he could. Jason figured if he still liked making beer after that year, it was the right fit.

Get a Pint

MCCOY'S PUBLIC HOUSE
St. Louis Park, Minnesota
mccoysmn.com

• • • •

MUDDY WATERS
Minneapolis, Minnesota
muddywatersmpls.com

• • • •

REPUBLIC
Minneapolis, Minnesota
republicmn.com

Jason and his wife talked about opening a brewery in 2001 and agreed Minneapolis would be a great place, but they didn't have the money. And even though he'd spent a year working at a professional brewery, Jason says he needed to learn more.

He went to study at the Siebel Institute in Chicago and Doemens Academy in Munich, Germany. In 2005 he began brewing at the Pelican Pub and Brewery in Pacific City, Oregon, working with the award-winning brewer Darron Welch. By the time Jason left four years later—he and his wife moved back to the Midwest to be near family after the birth of their daughter—he was head brewer.

By February 2011 Jason had started construction on his brewery. In August, he opened Steel Toe Brewing, a name inspired by his work as a toolmaker and the boots he wears.

The Beer

In the first years of the brewery, Jason has focused on making intense ales. He calls Provider a gateway into craft beer. "It's lighter in color—if it's dark, people think it's going to be really heavy—and there is just a little bitterness," he says. "It's a little lower alcohol, more approachable, but it has a lot more flavor and it's a lot more complex than a standard light lager."

Dissent, a dark ale, was named because "it's got its own opinion about what a dark beer should be," Jason says. While most stouts are full-bodied, Jason wanted to make his bold, but really drinkable.

Rainmaker, a hoppy red ale, came about when Jason was downhill mountain biking in Winter Park, Colorado. "It was a beautiful sunset up in the mountains, with that crisp pine scent in the air, and I thought that would be a great beer," Jason remembers.

The name of the trail he was riding all day was called Rainmaker.

Steel Toe's Size 7 IPA is a Northwest-style IPA, neatly organized by the number seven: 7 percent ABV, 77 IBUs, and pretty close to 7 SRM (Standard Reference Method: the system that specifies the color of beer).

Size 11 is Size 7's big brother. A triple IPA, it's 11 percent ABV, with 11 IBUs, at 11 SRM, and is released once a year as the brewery's winter seasonal. Other seasonals include an organic hefeweizen, Sommer Vice; the intensely malty Lunker, an English-style barley wine aged in rye whiskey barrels; and Before the Dawn, an unusual black barley wine aged in rye whiskey barrels. Jason says he's never actually seen a beer designated as a black barley wine. A cross between a barley wine and an Imperial stout, it's black in color and full of toffee and rich caramel flavors, without the big, roasty espresso often found in imperial stouts.

"All of the beers I make are beers that I really like," Jason says. That means really clean, not overly sweet and really well-attenuated—he focuses on malt and hops and prefers to brew beer without a lot of yeast or rye flavors.

In its first year, Steel Toe produced 150 barrels. In 2012 that number rose to 1,000

Steel Toe growlers are available
in the taproom.

and Jason opened a taproom to sell pints, but he says
he plans on keeping Steel Toe small.

"For me it's a quality issue; I'm a control freak,"
he says with a smile. "We always want to self-dis-
tribute, and that is the best way to keep track of the
beer and make sure it's being handled properly and is
always as fresh as it can be."

One unique way that Jason ensures such freshness
is bottling beer to order. The brewery takes orders
on Monday, fills bottles on Tuesday, and delivers on
Wednesday. For most of the liquor stores that Steel
Toe delivers to, the beer is no more than a day old, and
at most, a week. Jason says he tries to enter into agree-
ments with liquor stores that commit to keeping the
beer cold. When Steel Toe bottles, it bottles 22-ounce
bombers, two at a time, for a total output of 80 bottles
an hour.

"I think beer is incredibly perishable, especially
for very hoppy, moderate alcohol beers—mostly what
we do. It's important for it to be handled right," says
Jason, who wants to keep his beer extremely local and
available only in the Twin Cities.

"My dad built tractors for John Deere, and it was
always about supporting people in your community
and buying locally—it was better for everyone," Jason
says. Most of the brewery's equipment is second hand and repurposed; the equipment
he has purchased was made in the United States. "I think craft beer was intended to
be a local thing," he goes on. "The closer to home it is, the better it's going to be—
almost always."

BREWER'S PLAYLIST

PEARL JAM
- Porch

ALICE IN CHAINS
- Love Hate Love

METALLICA
- Creeping Death

PANTERA
- Domination

GRATEFUL DEAD
- Touch of Grey

KENNY CHESNEY
- On the Coast of
Somewhere Beautiful

STONE TEMPLE PILOTS
- Interstate Love Song

COUNTING CROWS
- Time and Time Again

MARRY POPPINS SOUNDTRACK
- Let's Go Fly a Kite
(for my daughter)

THE STAR-SPANGLED BANNER

CROSSROADS BARBERSHOP QUARTET
- Lucky Old Sun

WILLIE NELSON
- Whiskey River

ALISON KRAUSS & UNION STATION
- Lucky One

DAN FOGELBERG
- Leader of the Band (for my dad)

VIRTUE CIDER

FENNVILLE, MICHIGAN

'**ve** been asked by many people if I want to be the cider evangelist, and I say, 'That is a young man's job.' I did that with beer 20 years ago and that is nonstop hard work."

Greg Hall may reject the role of cider evangelist, but the role might have chosen him. With a 20-some-year history at Goose Island—Chicago's craft beer pioneer founded in 1988 by Greg and his father, John Hall, which recently sold to Anheuser-Busch InBev for $38.8 million—it seems hard to believe he is going to do cider without revolutionizing it, whether he intends to or not.

He's already started with the name itself: Virtue. Greg says he wanted to change the bad rap of the apple, associated with humanity's original vice. He wants to say that maybe apples aren't so bad.

"To me the apple tree is like Shel Silverstein's *Giving Tree*," Greg says. "You plant it once, it might need water for the first year or two but then never again, it cleans the air, holds the soil tight, provides shade, cools the planet, gives habitats for birds and beneficial insects: it's the most virtuous living thing on the planet."

From Beer to Cider

In 2000 Greg visited England with six other Goose Island brewers to visit as many different breweries and to explore

Owners
GREGORY HALL,
STEPHEN SCHMAKEL

Established
2011

Production Volume
24,000 GALLONS (2012)

Distribution
ILLINOIS
MICHIGAN
NEW YORK
OREGON

Website
virtuecider.com

as many different fermentation techniques as possible. They started in London and moved their way north. In Yorkshire, in the city of York, they went to a pub after a day of brewery visits. The pub was having a cider festival, and within the small pub, there was a wall of 40 gravity-fed casks of cider from all over the country.

Greg had always liked the idea of cider but had never found a cider that was as interesting to him as some of the beers he had had. The seven brewers tried half of the ciders that night. "Some were light and crisp, some dark and murky and sweet, some farm-y, some barrel-y, some so tannic it was like sucking on a Lipton tea bag," Greg remembers. They were so blown away by the range and complexity of flavors that they canceled their last brewery tour so they could return to The Maltings pub the next night and taste the other 20 ciders.

"We tried 40 ciders in two days and it was, to say the very least, life changing for me, because I knew someday I'd have to make cider," Greg says.

When Greg left Goose Island in 2011, he spent the summer on a cider pilgrimage and some time in the fall at Dupont in Normandy. When he returned home, he started pressing as much fruit as he could, using around 30 varieties from Nichols Farm & Orchard in Marengo, Illinois. He and his team tried around 24 different yeast strains, did 180 test batches, then blended those and tasted around 600 different ciders before settling on the recipe for Red Streak. Greg began contracting production at a winery in St. Julian, Michigan, and before a full year had passed since he left Goose Island, he released his first cider.

The Ciders

Red Streak is a blend of three ciders, each one fermented independently with different yeast and different apples and then blended together. A portion of that is aged in new American oak, which is then blended back in. "Red Streak is a perfect first release," Greg says. "It's a reintroduction to cider for a lot of people."

Red Streak is named after an apple that was developed in the 1600s by Lord Scudamore of Herefordshire, who was in the House of Lords. Greg tells the story as he knows it. Back then people in the country drank cider, the working class in the city drank ale, and the ruling class in the city drank French wine. The British were at war

Tanks filled with cider; a view of a landscape that will one day be filled with apple trees.

with the French, and it was Lord Scudamore—so the story goes—who pointed out that the British were buying materials from the enemy. His proposal was to craft the wine of the west: cider. He proposed that if he could make a cider as good as wine, British nobles would switch from drinking wine to drinking cider. He found an apple to make a great cider, called it the Red Streak, made the cider, carbonated it—years before Dom Pérignon came along—and brought it to the House of Lords. Greg says, while he doesn't know if it's fact or fable, Scudamore is attributed with the quote: "Before now, cider was a windy beverage for clowns and day laborers; with the Red Streak, it's now fit for kings, lords, and princes."

There are a lot of cider makers out there, but most are making a sweet colonial type of cider, he says. It isn't a good or bad style, he says, just a different one, and part of what Greg hopes to do is to educate the drinker on the many different styles of cider. At the Great American Beer Festival in Denver in 2012, there were 105 different categories for beer. Greg wants to create a cider association in hopes it might have a festival to showcase the variety of cider. In the year he launched Virtue, Greg said he had tasted as many as 400 ciders.

Sketches and designs for the Lapinette label and tap handle.

Lapinette, a French-style *cidre brut*, followed the release of Red Streak. It's made with acidic apples and is aged in French oak previously used in a California winery to age a range of different red wines. The cider picks up some of the character and color of the wine. Lapinette has more wood tones and more acidity to it than Red Streak, and it has a funkier flavor. Lapinette is named for the story of the French version of Groundhog

Empty apple crates on a snowy winter day—a reminder that cider is an agricultural product.

Day. In Normandy, Greg says, on the farms in spring, if there are young rabbits—*lapinettes*—in the orchards, it is a sign that there is going to be a good harvest, because the mother rabbit would not let her bunnies out of the hutch if another frost was coming.

The stories behind the ciders are an essential part of the process of planning and producing the ciders. It's all part of Virtue's craft. Not a step along the way lacks an intentional, artful touch.

Craft Cider

There are more than 20 states currently making cider with local apples. But because craft cider is an agricultural product tied closely to the land, the cider made in the United States is difficult to access. Greg wants to bring cider to the cider drinker in a broader context, while retaining the agricultural nature of the drink.

"It's unusual that cider holds the most natural place on the shelf and the least," Greg says, "You buy a beer, and you don't really look at the label: it's water, malt, hops, yeast. You buy a bottle of wine, you expect there to be grapes, maybe sulfites. With cider, what else would you possibly have in it besides apples and yeast?"

Greg pulls out four big-name American ciders; some that might seem more craft than others. Many of them have more than eight or nine ingredients, including apple juice concentrate, "the high fructose corn syrup of the fruit world," and caramel coloring.

The colors and flavors of Virtue's ciders come exclusively from the apples as they are harvested and pressed every fall and from the wood that houses them during aging. Greg uses many varieties of apples, and even those varieties change year to year. "Cider making is different from wine making or brewing in that you don't have

Get a Pint

HOPLEAF
Chicago, Illinois
hopleaf.com
• • • •
VILLAGE TAP
Chicago, Illinois
thevillagetap.com
• • • •
THE PUBLICAN
Chicago, Illinois
thepublicanrestaurant.com
• • • •
SALT OF THE EARTH
Fennville, Michigan
saltoftheearthfennville.com

specific recipes: you have apples," Greg says. "You don't sort them by pound or by apple or sometimes even by bin—it's what you get when you get it. You pick your apples, you mill them, you press them, you ferment the pressings, and then you produce your finished cider by blending at the end."

Virtue's tanks accept four pressings, and once the pressings are fermented, the cider makers blend to get the desired color, flavor, aroma, pH, and alcohol content.

Greg says ciders will vary much like a vintage dated wine, but even to a greater extent, because each harvest is different. "Some variability is what makes it a little

more agricultural," he says, "and that is one of the cool things that I really like about cider and the transition from brewing to cider."

Fennville

It isn't just apples and cider that Greg loves: he loves farms and farmers. Part of his model is to build a place that will support the local community of farmers, especially those who might not be able to get their product widely distributed otherwise.

Greg bought a 48-acre farm that was previously an orchard. A developer had bought it to create a subdivision and had cut all the trees down. Greg plans to plant trees and have his own fruit, and eventually around 10 percent of Virtue's cider will be made using fruit from the Fennville farm. The rest of the cider will continue to come from local farmers.

"We want people to drive up here and think, 'I'm in Normandy—I can't believe this is Michigan,'" he says. His plans don't end with the beautiful Norman-style cider houses, which hold the fermenters and juice tanks. Future plans include a barrel room, a café, a formal garden and three caves: one for cider, one for cheese, and one for pork.

"We want to be the Stone Barns of the Chicago area," says Greg. "In 10 years we'd love to have a community of artisanal farmers and food producers in southwest Michigan who then can easily deliver to the major markets of Chicago, Grand Rapids, Detroit, and Indianapolis."

His focus is cider, but for Greg it's about so much more. He even has ambitions to change his agricultural neighbors. Near his Fennville farm are half a dozen pig farms—enclosed barns and windowless cinder block operations. "My idea is to say, 'You're raising 500 pigs and getting 60 cents a pound. I'll pay you three or four bucks a pound if you do it this way. Start by doing a few pigs the other way, and see how much easier and cleaner it is.'"

Once an evangelist, always an evangelist.

BREWER'S PLAYLIST

ARCHERS OF LOAF • Web in Front
BANANAS • Nautical Theme
BEIRUT • Postcards from Italy
ERIN TOBEY • Robot Song
ERIN TOBEY • Psychology Song
ERIN TOBEY • Relativity Song
DANIEL JOHNSTON • Girlfriend
JARVIS COCKER • Fantastic Mr. Fox AKA Petey's Song
MODEST MOUSE • Sleepwalking
THE CONCRETES • Chosen One
FEELIES • Crazy Rhythms
HANDSOME FAMILY • Giant of Illinois
THE JAZZ BUTCHER • Partytime
JOHN HUSS • Rockin' at a Hyde Park Party
JONATHAN RICHMAN • South American Folk Song
WACO BROTHERS • Take Me to the Fires
WILCO • I'm Always in Love
TOM WAITS • Martha
MATT & KIM • Cinders
MOUNTAIN GOATS • Narakaloka

MOODY TONGUE BREWING COMPANY

CHICAGO, ILLINOIS

e work in different environments, have different hours, and brewers get to intoxicate people, but otherwise chefs and brewers are basically the same people," says Jared Rouben, co-owner of the new Moody Tongue Brewing Company.

    With that in mind, Jared is creating a brewery where cooking and brewing are inextricably linked: a brewery that he defines as a *culinary-driven* brewery. To Jared that means beers inspired by food, using artisanal ingredients—spices, farmers' market produce, and things you might expect to find in a kitchen and not on the shelves of a brewery.

Before he was a brewer, and well before he was the brewmaster at Chicago's Goose Island Brewery, Jared was a cook. He cooked at a restaurant in Napa and then at Per Se, Thomas Keller's three-Michelin-starred restaurant in New York.

In his first week as a student at the Culinary Institute of America (CIA) in New York, Jared started a beer club. "At the end of my shifts cooking, we weren't drinking Chardonnay and Malbec," he says. "We were drinking pilsners and IPAs and pale ales. I thought, these are the people who are creating these beautiful dishes—we should pay attention: this is their beverage of choice."

For the CIA beer club, which still exists today, Jared brought in beer from breweries across the northeast—Ommegang, Sam

---

Owners
JARED ROUBEN,
JEREMY COHN

Brewmaster
JARED ROUBEN

Established
2013

Production Volume
2,400 BARRELS (EST.)

Distribution
ILLINOIS

Website
moodytongue.com

Adams, Dogfish Head—and the students would cook, bake, and pair with beer. The chef–brewer connection was there for Jared from the beginning.

In 2007 Jared moved to Chicago to attend the Siebel Institute of Technology, which took him to Germany. When he had finished his schooling, Jared applied to 65 breweries and brewpubs across the country via snail mail, email, and phone calls. Of 65, he was rejected by 64. He took the one job he was offered, at Rock Bottom Brewery in Warrenville, Illinois. He worked there for a year, until the economy fell apart and the brewery let go of all of its assistants.

It wasn't the worst thing to happen to him: three days later, he got hired by Goose Island. Eleven months after that, he was hired as its brewmaster. It was a fast turnaround, from new employee to brewmaster in less than a year, but Jared was extremely focused, and Goose Island was receptive to his interest in food-driven beer.

He began to pursue the bridging of cooks and brewers that had been on his mind since the CIA, and he started a Chef Collaboration series. He sent out emails to 35 CIA chefs in Chicago about doing a beer collaboration, and six months later got his first response: a rejection. "At that point, I was a little used to rejection," Jared jokes, "and I didn't give up on it, I really thought we had something special here."

Then Jared met Rob and Ali Leavitt, then the chef-owners of Mado in the Bucktown neighborhood of Chicago and today the owners of the artisanal, locally focused, whole-animal butcher shop The Butcher & Larder.

"Boy, was I happy I came across them, because they were friends with the chef at Goose Island, John Manion, and they were interested in brewing," Jared says. "Ali is an amazing baker, and Rob just enjoys beer and the process." He brought them in and made the first Chef Collaboration beer, an imperial witbier called White City that ended up being mass-produced by Goose Island, one of the most successful chef collaborations of the 54 Jared went on to brew.

Jared's goal was to create hyper-focused, handcrafted beers tailored to each chef and his or her restaurant. His process included eating at the restaurant; researching the chef; and having a sit-down conversation where the guest chef and Jared tasted beers and found the direction they would go in terms of color, aromatics, flavor, and alcohol.

Then the chefs—100 percent of them participated—would go to the brewery with Jared and spend the eight or nine hours it took to make the beer.

Initially Jared approached the chefs, but soon they started coming to him. "Each chef had a different focus, and each could tell me exactly what they wanted," Jared says. "For some, it was what made sense with their food, others might come in and say they wanted a really hoppy beer."

Some knew precisely what they wanted, like Frontera Grill's Rick Bayless. "He said, 'Jared, I want this to go with ceviche and guacamole, I want it to be light and refreshing, and I don't want you to dumb it down: I want there to be layers of flavor,'" Jared says. Together they created Marisol, the most successful beer in the Chef Collaboration Series and one of the most rewarding beers he crafted while at Goose Island. "It was the most difficult and the most rewarding," he says. "It's approachable and complex, and those are difficult things to put together."

The beers created with the chefs were available at the brewpub as well as at the chef's restaurant. Jared offered a guarantee to the chefs: if they didn't like the finished product, they didn't have to take it. Not one of the 54 chefs turned it down.

"I wouldn't be able to get there without their skill and talent as well," Jared says. "As a brewer, bringing in a chef who is an expert with his palate opened my mind—to different ingredients and different resources."

Farmers' Market Series

Working with chefs opened Jared's mind to different ingredients and different places to source those ingredients. "With beer you are such a minimalist: water, barley, hops, yeast, and then maybe an additional ingredient," Jared says. Wanting to make every ingredient count, Jared asked chefs where they got their spices, and soon he was ordering spice from Terra Spice. He asked where they sourced their food, and soon he was shopping weekly at Green City Market, Chicago's largest market for local and sustainable food.

"I'd been going to the market for selfish reasons, just because it was delicious," Jared says, "but at that point I thought, why am I ordering online from a brewer's catalogue when I can go to Green City Market just blocks away?"

He began going to the market with beer in mind, talking to the farmers, who eventually began to grow specialty items for him, like a chocolate habanero pepper, and would alert him when the first blueberries or raspberries were in season.

"That was such a turning point for me because that gave my beer that extra layer of flavor," Jared says. The market opened up endless possibilities: applewood honey, baby carrots, fresh lavender, pumpkin—there were so many things for Jared to use in what became a weekly farmers' market beer. Jared brewed one keg that highlighted an ingredient from one farm, and it was available at the brewpub until it was gone.

He used ingredients and flavors he'd previously never considered when crafting beer, but he was also wary of extreme experimentation with his farmers' market beers. "These beers had to be delicious—not just a talking point," Jared says. "At the end of the day the beer should be tasty, and that is always my goal."

Opening a Brewery

At the beginning of 2013, news was traveling fast across the city that Jared Rouben, ex-brewmaster at Goose Island, was planning his own brewery.

Jared says he had been planning it in some form since he was at the CIA, with his first innovation of the beer club. "It wasn't until now that I felt like I was ready. I really wanted to hone my craft," Jared says. "And I was never going to do anything before I felt like I could make something special." With the market so saturated, Jared says he wouldn't start a brewery if he didn't feel he was creating something different.

In the early months before Jared had fully released the details of his Chicago brewery-to-be, the foundation of what he would do was clear: hyper-seasonal beers that incorporated the best ingredients available—whether that meant beautiful cherries from a farmer or artisanal honey from a beekeeper.

Intentionality was another focus: everything he does, Jared says, will have a reason. "Do you ever go to a restaurant and get a plate where they have the little green parsley around the outside? That will never happen at my brewery," he says. "Everything will have a purpose to make it better, not to make it pretty."

Jared says the brewery, which he opened with his cousin, Jeremy Cohn, won't offer a series of one-off beers; he plans to perfect the recipes of the beers he makes. He wants his beers to be approachable—if customers like your beer, he says, they're going to buy it. He's already thinking about his customers at the stage when he's writing recipes for his beers. "Remember, you're only as good as your last beer," he says.

"It's easy to throw a lot of ingredients in and say, 'Wow, I created something,'" Jared says. "It's a lot more difficult to envision what you're going to create beforehand and actually follow through and do it."

BREWER'S PLAYLIST

DAVID BOWIE
- Golden Years

RANDY TRAVIS
- A Few Ole Country Boys

SAM COOKE • A Change Is Gonna Come

NEIL DIAMOND
- Kentucky Woman

RAY CHARLES
- Georgia on My Mind

WAYLON JENNINGS WITH WILLIE NELSON
- Good Hearted Woman

MIRANDA LAMBERT
- Airstream

LOUIS ARMSTRONG
- La Vie En Rose

WILLIE NELSON AND WAYLON JENNINGS
- Mama Don't Let Your Babies Grow Up to Be Cowboys

STEVIE WONDER
- Superstition

ACKNOWLEDGMENTS

····

Many thanks to my brewers, my publisher and editors, and my family.

INDEX

····

ABOUT THE AUTHOR

Anna Blessing is the author and photographer of *Locally Grown: Portraits of Artisanal Farms from America's Heartland* as well as 14 editions of the eat.shop/rather city guides. She lives in Chicago with her husband and daughter.